Miss Teacher Mom

Written by Katlynne Mirabal · Illustrated by Timerie Blair

No part of this book may be reproduced or transmitted in any form or by any means without written permission from MissTeacherMomPublishing@gmail.com.

Katlynne Mirabal
Blair

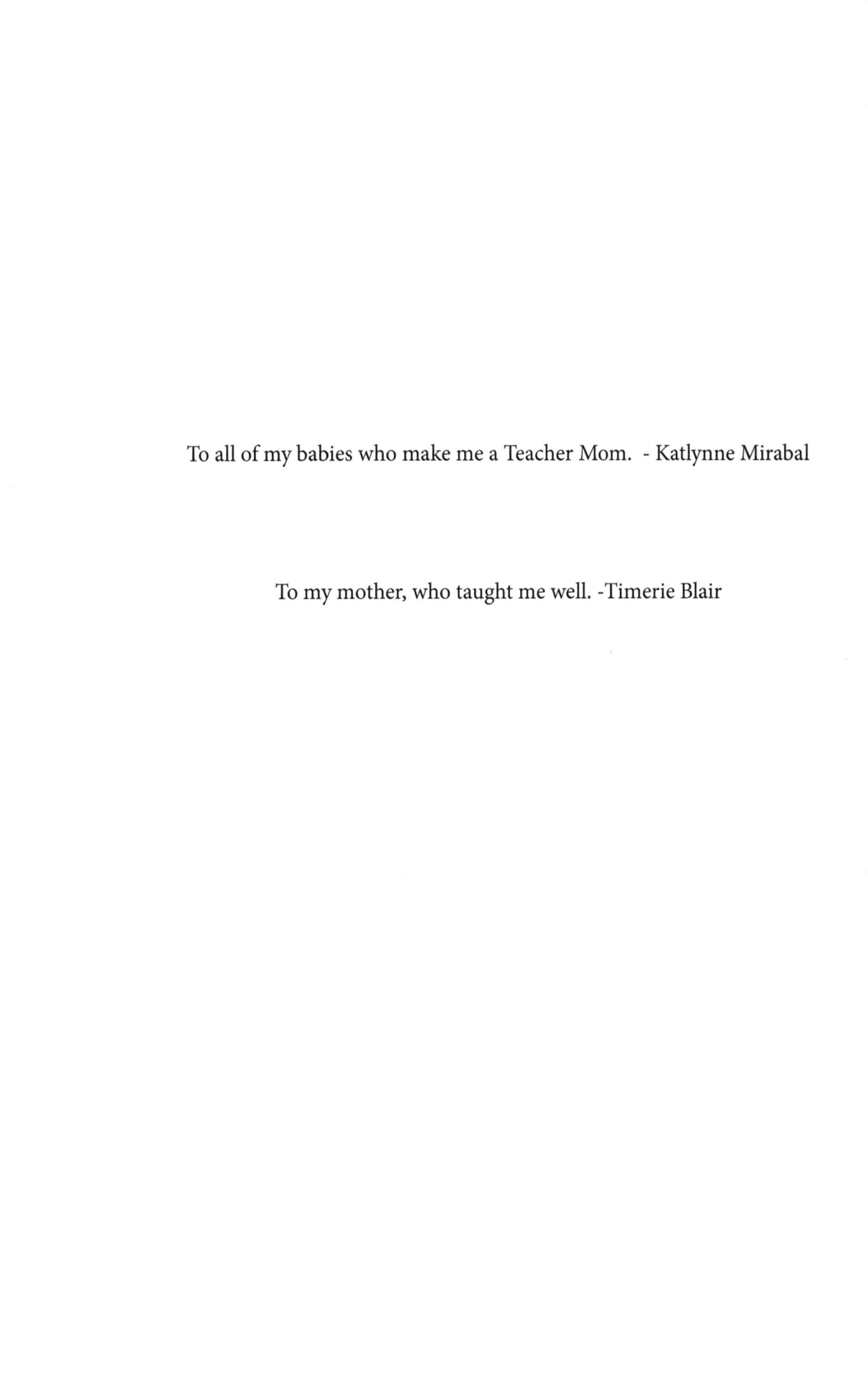

To all of my babies who make me a Teacher Mom. - Katlynne Mirabal

To my mother, who taught me well. -Timerie Blair

I wake up in the mornin

and jump out of bed.

Today is a school day with Momma again!

She brushes my teeth,

and combs my hair.

She lets me pick out the clothes I'll wear.

Miss momma makes every

day so much fun!

We laugh and we snuggle.

We dance and we jump.

he books.

And we sing all the songs.

We

make

lots of

messes

with   Miss   Teacher   M

She's beautiful, patient, lovely and kind.

Of all the teachers, I'm glad she's mine.

e my numbers, my letters and more.

We hang my work on the freezer door.

When nighttime comes and she tucks me in bed,

I look forward to morning to see her again!

Taking Back YOUr Right to Live Heaven on Earth

*Ignite YOUr Heart
Embrace YOUr Awareness
Embody YOUr Truth*

Transcending Through Sacred Poetry

Agatha Fallone Cretaro

◆ FriesenPress

One Printers Way
Altona, MB R0G 0B0
Canada

www.friesenpress.com

Copyright © 2024 by Agatha Fallone Cretaro
First Edition — 2024

Illustration Credits are given to Melissa Young for her reproductions of all images given to me by God for the purpose of Divine visual meanings and concepts.

All rights reserved.

No part of this publication may be reproduced in any form, or by any means, electronic or mechanical, including photocopying, recording, or any information browsing, storage, or retrieval system, without permission in writing from FriesenPress.

ISBN
978-1-03-917527-3 (Hardcover)
978-1-03-917526-6 (Paperback)
978-1-03-917528-0 (eBook)

1. SELF-HELP, MOTIVATIONAL & INSPIRATIONAL

Distributed to the trade by The Ingram Book Company

The Greatest love there is, Self_Love shines the brightest
A beacon of shimmering white light cascading onto us,
Building a circumference of strength around us
Profound Love realized from the Heart not the mind
Discovering YOUr true sense of BEing,
Leads you to the deepest of LOVE there is,
YOU_GOD = Self_Love
Anchored in Trust, Faith, Belief of YOU

Table of Purposeful Contents

Dedication to My Father xi

Giving Thanks xv

BEfore YOUr Reading Journey xix

Openness–Preparing To Be ME 1
    The Evolutionary Self 2
    Self_Love 4
    Semantics of Truth 5
    Relinquish Control 6
    Sitting in Silence 7
    In Unity of Thyself 8
    Letting Go 9
    Rebirthing 10
    Spiritual Journey 11
    Sensory Observations 12
    Survivorship 13
    Living Peace 15
    Our Voices 16
    Me 18

Ignite YOUr Heart 19
    FAITH of SELF 21
    Divinely YOU 23
    Discovery 24
    Acknowledgement of the Soul 25
    A Prayer for YOUr Soul 26
    Free Will Activation 27
    Transcending into YOU 28

Beautiful YOU 29
Acceptance with Purpose 30
Beautiful Eyes 32
Depths of Gratitude 33
Made of YOU 34
Reflective ME, Age 17 35
Self BEcoming 36
The Absence of Truth 37
Scope of LOVE 38
The LOVE Beneath YOU 39
Learning to Trust SELF 40
When Sadness Grows 42
People I Love 43
Choices 44
Celebrate YOUr Life 45
Just Because YOU Can 47
Sacred Body 50
Welcoming YOU 51
Fun, Play, Laughter 52

Embrace YOUr Awareness 55

Silent Night 58
Overcoming 60
Sacred Bond 61
In the Shadows 62
My Worth is to ME 64
No Regrets 65
Acceptance of the Rising YOU 66
Blue Sky and the Sea 67
Drifting White Clouds 68
Peeling Back Self-Doubt 69
Rising Anger 71
Rainbow of Truth 72
God's Intent for ME 75
Healing Words from God 77
The Act of Forgiveness 78
The Warrioress 80
Taking Back MY Right 82
To My Wounded Self 84
Praising Actions of Within 85
Worthy of Forgiveness 86

YOU, In The Present Moment 88
Parts of ME 90
Imparting YOU 91
Spirited You 92
Tremendous Degree of Peace 93
Healing Sounds of Summer 94
Living Your Humanness on this Earth 96

Embody YOUr Truth 99

Calling Back My Truth 101
Grounding for Life Pays off in Dividends 103
Flow 104
A State of BEing 106
Creating a NEW Life For You 107
Expiring Thoughts 108
I'm Not Afraid 109
Mirror, Mirror on the Wall 110
My Story of Truth 111
Regaining Yourself 112
Divine Feminine Energy within Everyone 114
Riding the Wings of Change 116
I Shall Prevail 117
Gift of Life 119
On This Earthy Plain 120
Most at Peace 122
Ego's Transformation 123
Expression of YOU 124
The Mother In Me 125
Exercising YOUr Right 126
I Love My Son 128
My Soulmate 129
The Love between Us 130
Those you Love 131
The Love for My Children 132
Trusting 133
The Power To BE 134
Loving YOUr Self Through and Through 135
Earthly Elements 136
Viable Strength 138
Thankful 140
Spectrum of Your Soul 141

Practicing the Lessons 144
　　Tree of Life 146

Continuance—The Evolution Never Ends 149

　　Your Reality 150
　　Rejoicing Love 151
　　Sustainable YOU 153
　　Nature_ME 154
　　I am ME 155
　　The Truth of NOW 156
　　The Progression of YOU 157
　　Understanding 158
　　Words from God to You 159
　　YOU_GOD 161
　　The Divine would Say 163
　　Smile Till It Hurts 164
　　Mountain_Ocean 165
　　Within ME 166
　　A New Day 167
　　On a Rainy Day 169
　　Our Community 170
　　Holding Kindness for Another 171
　　Your Tribe 172
　　You are Called 174

BEfore I Leave You 177

Dedication to My Father

Profound sentiments rise
As I acknowledge my father from the other side
Standing by my side, never leaving my side
His death was the catalyst for my enlightenment
Propelling me where I am today
Not realizing at the time, what was in store for ME,
The depths of My Evolution
Tears swell to my human eyes as I write this poem
Needing to release my deep LOVE for him
In complete Peace as I do
Knowing he is still watching over ME, in past lives and many more to come
Understanding his spiritual purpose, influencing mine
While alive and in the after life
Forever part of My Spiritual Family

I Thank You, Dad
For complying as you needed to BE
Because of YOU,
Your dedication to ME
This Sacred Poetry Book is made possible
For others to aspire and transpire as they need to BE
As prescribed by the Heavens

Forever and For Always,
ME_YOU_GOD

Giving Thanks

To My Family

Evolution Through Peace

My transformation into ME
Graceful and clean
Learning to BE ME
Was and still is, my Spiritual Journey on God's Green Earth
Attributed to my Spiritual Contract
Those dedicated to ME, as I am to them
My Earthly family, loving me unconditionally
Assisting me along my path, to BEcome ME
Learning the Depths of ME
Transpiring as God has prescribed ME to BE
Tremendous Gratitude, expelling through Holy Tears as I write…
Profound Love within my Sacred Heart, beyond words can describe
Forever and for always, in Love with my Earthly Family
On this Earth and Beyond…

As our spiritual connections transcribes into the Heavens
We learn how to heal ourselves here, on Earth, because of our bond
Dedication to each other, we grow into ourselves as we need to BE,
We BEcome, learning what it is we came here to learn
On different paths, united here, we grow together as separate BEings
Beautiful relationships I do not take for granted
Giving thanks to your commitment to my growth, as I am to yours
Loving you with all of ME, the depths of ME at a cellular level
Thank you, as I 'see' you standing before ME,
Loving me back, with the Grace of God coming through all of you now
I feel this Love, your Love, from your Holy Selves. . .

Elevating through this Loving Exchange. . . I pause. . . taking a deep breath. . . exhaling. . .

I AM committed to Loving you humanly, and spiritually
For all the days of my earthy life, and beyond…

Me_Family_God

To My Mentors

Deepest Gratitude to my mentors
Prolific BEings to ME
Energized by God's Graces
Dedicated to BE, examples of BEing
As I'm evolving to BE; how God needs me to BE
Vessels translating God's Truth to ME
Exactly how I needed to hear
In the precise moment of time
I receive God's Healing Energy; God teaching ME
Sharing their Holy Selves with me, on demand
Wisdom, I will forever cherish, adore, and respect
Knowing I will pay it forward as God prescribes me to BE
As my mentors have done with ME
Beyond my mind can comprehend
The Love between US
I know, there are reasons beyond what I need to know
So, I choose
I will continue to proceed
What I need to BE. . .

Thank you.

Before Your Reading Journey

My Writing Inspiration

Understand the Divine is genderless, faceless, formless and nameless to me. ITs presence is grand, deep in depth and width and bright. Very bright. I am hypersensitive to this Divine presence as I am part of IT (and so are you). Over the years, I have learned how to recognize the signs the Divine uses to help me heal through forgiveness leading to a sacred path of revealing, healing and adopting my authentic self as I live my human life on Earth. As I work through self-editing this Book, aligning and realigning my non-poetry words and preparing it for its release, it is clear that my purpose for writing is to share Divine Wisdom with the reader. My writing inspiration flowing through me is Divine's Grace putting down on paper in a particular way for the reader the words needed to guide them to *Ignite*, *Embrace* and *Embody* their authentic selves as IT has done with me. By sharing the book, I am doing my part in God's bigger plan in working with humanity. As I have learned to TRUST, have FAITH and BELIEVE in this Higher Power within me, my writing inspiration is expressed in many ways, through drawings, journaling and now through poetry.

The overarching inspiration of this Sacred Poetry Book comes from the Divine's Grace found within me, forming my dedication to self-discovery through profound spiritual healings. The Law of Forgiveness is my means for healing occurring at a spiritual level within my awareness of the greater part of ME. My sacred journey, both intense and beautiful to say the least, has taught me for sustainable happiness to be achieved, forgiveness is the key to life. My sacred journey to healing misconceptions, revealing my truest essence, and understanding I am the Divine allows me to remain true to my earthly purpose. Found in this Book of Grace are the very words the Divine used as IT guided me (and continues to guide me) through my forgiveness healing journey. When I reread my poetry, I swell up with love and gratitude, reigniting the heavenly sentiments I first experienced. Designed as reminders of learned meanings, all I can do is exhale and say "Thank You" . . . bowing my head, expelling sacred tears. Bring me back to my center, where Peace and Grace are found, keep me grounded within ME and propel me further into ME.

Sometimes, Divine inspiration comes from a word or phrase someone said or something I was guided to read. Directing me to look out my window, sit on my deck, or the even mantras the Divine gives me during meditation leads me to write. Whatever resonates within my core, I know it will have a deeper meaning, and I need to express it on paper. I often hear the word "write," "we want you to write," or "write this down." So, I do it without thought. Exactly, without thought or without my ego. Never in control of what words come out, sitting in complete TRUST, FAITH and BELIEF within my Holy Self in solidarity with the Divine.

When I sit down with my laptop on my legs, not knowing what will transpire on paper, I know it will be beautiful. Sometimes, I ask for clarity as the flow isn't resonating with me, and I struggle through it. Remember, I'm healing in real time as I write. I hear: "remember this," or "reread from the beginning," or "We want to take it this way," or I get visions flash in my mind's eye of learned awareness to help me through it. Some poems are completed at different times, days even months apart. Sometimes, I start poems, get part way, and then the words stop coming. I hear, "another time," or "leave it for now," or "you are done for now". Eventually, I would hear nothing, another indication I needed to leave it. I am always guided back to the unfinished poem. As a continuation of my healing articulating, in a precise Divine manner, the layered awareness of Self I was learning. Beautifully capturing the desired meaning and impact comes directly from a sacred place of understanding. Now brought to you to assist you through YOUr sacred journeys, I call Spirituality.

These sacred words are simple, but their meanings are not. Word arrangements may cause confusion or even frustration, which is ok, for it is a sign that healing is necessary. Each poem has layered meanings, more profound than the one on top of it, like peeling back an onion to get to the core of YOU. What you get out of it depends on you. Your dedication to Self is your commitment to make. Free will plays a big part. Just know the Divine is also within you, as you are IT as well. IT is guiding you. It is up to you to take notice. This Sacred Poetry Book is here for you as the Divine intends: wanting all of us to connect with IT, so *we can all take back our right to live Heaven on Earth*.

How To Use This Sacred Poetry Book

This Sacred Poetry Book came into existence quickly, indicating the need for God's Wisdom to transcend among those needing guidance to a new life. Humanity is plagued with so much suffering. We are stuck in old programing and harbouring unfair expectations. We are surrendering to our suffering, accepting it to be our truth! Every day, people struggle within themselves; it is constant as if this state of being is normal. It doesn't have to be this way! This Book is designed to guide the reader through the Law of Forgiveness healing practice. The concept of healing is, by nature free flowing and directional once the reader connects to their inner voice or intuition; it is always based on God's Truth anchored within everyone. There is no wrong or right way to heal; the reader's healing process forms their spiritual path according to God's will. There is no judgement in their sacred healing journeys. Healing is self-directed, made up of personal actions, and results will vary according to what is meant for the person actively transcending. What you need from this Sacred Poetry Book will resonate with you. Be open to the signs. Divinely inspiring words to uplift you when you are down, encouraging you to move forward positively and learn how to love yourself. Interpretation of these sacred words is for you to flow into. Through healing, understanding rises as you experience the forgiveness healing unfold and ponder what this means to you. The journey is not a destination, and there are no limits of any kind as this journey is free flowing as you need to be. The time is now to *Take Back YOUr Right to Live Heaven on Earth*.

Openness - Preparing to BE ME

This chapter reveals the need to be ready to do your healing work. Relaxing the mind encourages openness to activate free will to be ready. The chapter introduces the reader to spiritual concepts outlining the benefits of fulfilling healing work. Are you ready to seek a better way of living? Are you ready to learn how to become a better version of yourself? To be ready means, you are willing to accept all of you, whatever that happens to be for you. It is the beginning of learning to trust yourself, even in the presence of fear.

Ignite your Truth

This chapter supports you through your fear (and any other negative sentiment) of self-exploration. Acknowledging rising apprehension, you decide to proceed with your self-discovery anyway, seeking God's Wisdom along the way. It is the beginning of learning how to trust, have faith and belief in yourself to preserver through the pain. Learning to find one's inner voice, recognizing innate intuition then learning to trust this internal source of Grace starts to become present. Feeling the rising love within you will assist with grounding means from Grace.

Embrace your Awareness

This chapter continues you on your path of self-discovery. Revealing deeper parts of you as you face your fears and actively transmuting them into your light by means of the Law of Forgiveness healing practice. You are empowered through the realization of your deeper self, and you are coming into alignment with your Light, Power and Authority your essence holds. These Keys of Life are not lost, as you will realize. You are starting to step into your awareness as BEing your Holy Self, whatever this state of BEing means to you.

Embody your Truth

This chapter takes you deeper into self-discovery by learning how to BE. Now starting to understand your truth, this is the part you explore ways to live within your exalted Self. Shifting into your new BEing means thinking, saying, and acting in finite ways, keeping you grounded within your superior BEing. This is a process of humility: viable actions taking you out of your old ways, leading you into your new ways of BEing and initiating more healing opportunities.

Continuance - The Evolution Never Ends

Your sacred evolution never ends. This chapter opens your observations to other Divine connections linking YOU to your communities and environment. More self-discovery can be gained as you live life from the perspective of the new SELF. Expanding your broader perspective and applying it to your day-to-day will bring you more "ah ha" moments, leading you deeper within YOU.

This Book is outlined in this manner to gently guide the reader through the Law of Forgiveness healing practice for the purpose of living a joyous life. Forgiveness reclaims ownership of the Keys of Life as one takes back their right to live Heaven on Earth. This Sacred Poetry Book opens the readers' minds to the concept of forgiveness and the means of forgiving. Applying the Law of Forgiveness at a spiritual level requires the reader to find their intuition and learn how to work within their innate wisdom. Igniting, embracing and embodying truth is about becoming one with their innate wisdom. The stages outlined here don't always flow this logically. You may repeat the self-discovery steps in a different order for your deeper awareness to surface. The perceived struggle from one step to the other is part of the journey as you persevere through confusion and doubt, one issue at a time. Remember, healing is happening at a spiritual level, so healing transcends the time and space our minds are accustomed to experiencing. The journey of self-discovery or awareness is learning how to convert the ego mind, where suffering is planted, into living within your Sacred Self, where love, joy and bliss are planted. This conversion is called healing and is a very gentle process where you foster innate courage found within yourself. This beautiful courage leads you to your innate wisdom of TRUST, FAITH and BELIEF of YOU_GOD.

The Poems in this Book represent my personal healing journey at an infinite level. The Divine gave me the words to write to share ITs wisdom with YOU, as I've used them to learn the depths of ME. The healing journey can start off difficult, and wanting to quit will be present as I've experienced these very natural human sentiments. Do not judge yourself. Remember, any level of peace you experience by simply reading God's words is the source of your continuance to achieving GRACE.

This Sacred Poetry Book is for you wherever you are on your spiritual awakening path. Your path is about discovering YOU, and it is not about comparing your path or the success of each step. This approach is a mental exercise applied to a spiritual process. It doesn't work this way. Healing is a personal journey, a sacred bond forming one's spirituality. Spirituality is the discovery of one's beautiful, loving and joyous relationship with God; *achieving oneness with God is living Heaven on Earth*.

Understanding My Writing Lens

You achieve unity with the Power to BE through YOUr journey of self-discovery, an infinite understanding, and a path of exclusive means to uncovering, healing, and BEcoming God. *Living Heaven on Earth* is a lifelong dedication to self; rebuilding the Soul is a graceful act of SELF_LOVE. Self_Love starts to flourish once you understand the interrelationship, cause and effect, of all your parts: spirit, body, and mind. The integration of your parts, working together to produce YOU, is part of the spiritual journey of discovery. This integration happens at a spiritual awareness utilizing the Law of Forgiveness, shedding what isn't you and building up what is you. Never in a straight line, one's sacred journey is their Divine plan. In this Book, Divine's Grace guides the reader to the Law of Forgiveness healing practice through inspirational and motivational sequencing of Divine Energy through ITs words. Some poetry speaks to you from these parts separately, in verses guiding you to understanding forgiveness. Self-discovery is a choice based on a trigger(s) for the need for a fulfilled life on earth. This Sacred Poetry Book introduces the reader to the concept of forgiveness, broadening awareness of this graceful act of healing, one step at a time, through Divine steps of *Igniting, Embracing and Embodying one's truth for the purpose of living Heaven on Earth.*

In my state of BEing, I am sitting in union with God when I write, fully conscious of ME. I'm in a deep, relaxed state of bliss where PEACE is my resident sentiment. My spirit, body and mind are all aligned with the Divinity within me and therefore entirely open for TRUTH to funnel through all parts of me, then, I transcribe God's intention for you (as it was for me) into words. The Higher Power guides me to write precisely, outlining spiritual themes, concepts, and meanings. I hear the Divine whispering in my ear the very words to use, and IT is adamant I do not change these words unless I'm guided to do so. I do not question what I'm writing; I simply write. How these sacred words are organized on the page is Divinely purposeful. Hence the term Sacred Poetry. Each word is delicate, sequenced beautifully, with transcending meaning, carrying Divine Energy designed to help you *Take Back Your Right to Live Heaven on Earth.*

Everything about the Book is Divinely guided: its premise, layout of chapters, poem placements, and images. Word choices and the visual representation of words and, therefore, their meanings are all intentional with Divine meaning. These poems are designed to create wonder and encouragement for deeper exploration of their meaning for you. Making the assessments individual and deeply personal is precisely what God intends. You may be guided to return to a poem, ascertaining a completely different meaning than the first time you read it, providing a more profound understanding layered onto the first meaning you received. Sometimes, rereading a poem brings profound confidence in ITs intent for you. Brilliant! This is how the Divine works.

I have to admit; my human self was tempted to interpret these Sacred Words from my own healed perspective in an attempt to make the understanding of this Book more effective for you. I've personally struggled to want to clarify the intended reading style and word interpretation the Divine has given me. I have learned on my journey of producing my first Sacred Poetry Book; it isn't up to me to give my interpretation! I am a vessel sharing God's LIGHT through ITs words. Spirit told me: ". . .You are not required to explain the whole premise at this time. So, relax into US, and we will continue to guide YOU accordingly. . ." With this message, I stepped back into my TRUTH. I infinitely know the Divine is guiding you already, leading you to your infinite understanding based on your awareness journey.

Before this work, I have never written poetry. Now, it is one of many ways the Divine communicates with me. As I travel deeper on my spiritual path, various creative methods enhance exponentially. When I started writing, I had no idea what would transpire or even know publishing a book was the goal until I got to the point of knowing. I trusted what was happening because of the profound insights that followed after I understood each poem's meaning. My understanding unfolded as I wrote the poems. The healing impact, equally profound, helped me develop new perspectives on life, overturning old beliefs. Living in a constant space of peace, comfort, and calm is living Heaven on Earth. My faith grew at the same speed as the words flowed out of me. Witnessing my rising self emerge into my Holy Self, uniting with the Divine directly, from these sacred words, fueled my belief in Self_Love. Understanding this growth is ongoing, I have dedicated my human life to BEcoming the best version of ME.

My Sacred Duty

I write sacred poetry
As I connect with my Holy Self
Resembling the larger part of ME
I transcribe the sentiments
Flowing through me to you
Articulating the Scope of Reverie
Profoundly capturing Divine Essence
Describing in finite ways
To BE on this Earth

To BE on this Earth
Is to live Heaven on Earth
Without fear, shame, guilt. . .
Without any other egoic rituals
We are programed to feel, and have adopted

It is our purpose
To take back our Right
To live Heaven on Earth

And as we do
Learning the lessons
We committed to learning
Before coming to Earth
We owe it to ourselves
To live out our journeys
For the purpose of transcendence
Transcending, getting closer to Source

Soul growth, is maturity you have never known
Assisting us, in this current life, on this Earth
Living to BE sustainable
Foundationally grounded on Mother Earth
Without being knocked to our knees
Getting up in our Resiliency
Preforming Miracles on Earth
As you practice BEing
Transcending, getting closer to GOD

Articulating the Essence of God
Profoundly assisting me
With my Sacred Evolution,
Of My Essence, on this Earth
Describing the hurt felt
How to over come
With the Law of Forgiveness
Guidance attributed to Source
Empowering My Essence
To evolve according to plan

As I BE on this Earth
I will continue to write Sacred Poetry
For You_ME

Openness—
Preparing To Be ME

The Evolutionary Self

Just be. . .here

Observing you
With all of your senses
Without judgement
Igniting your Heart
Of what comes
As it comes
You accept what is
Performing life's riches
Understanding your scope of reverie
Is bountiful beyond salaries
Riches of YOU
A discovery of worthiness
Worth more than the mind can conceive
A sentiment worth exploring
As you BEcome
YOU

Just be. . .here

Profound Love rising
Learning what this means
Spirituality of YOU, birthing
Comprehension expanding
Enveloping the new YOU
As you discover deeper of YOU
Embracing your awareness
Healing the unhealed parts of you
Working through all parts of you
With patience,
With Love,
With tenacity,
With perseverance,
Pulling yourself through
Working with the Larger part of YOU
Prevailing as you heal
Learning the new YOU
Each time you do

As you BEcome
YOU

Just be. . .here

Profound Love rising still
Even deeper than before
Seeing what you don't see
Knowing it is what's needed
For sustainability
Accepting the new YOU
Living as the new YOU
Is learning how to
Embody your Truth
Practicing BEing is the Journey
Living in a United state
Soul_God
Every minute of the day
Never going back to the old you
Celebration of Truth
Not wanting anything else
Other than

Just BEing. . .here

Self_Love

Exploring Truth takes Courage

Exploring Truth takes Compassion

Exploring Truth takes Kindness

Exploring Truth takes Trust

Exploring Truth takes Faith

Exploring Truth takes Belief

Exploring Truth takes You_ME

The Divine will say…

Semantics of Truth

Semantics is a human requirement
On the other side, there are no labels
Just profound
LOVE

Whatever we decide to call the Divine:
God, Universe, Unified Field, Love, Infinity . . .
Soul_Love
Spirit_God
Spirit_Christ
Christ_God
Soul_Nature
Nature_God
God_Mother Earth
Everything_Everything

God speaks to us in specific ways
Ways, we will resonate with IT
Sole purpose is to unite with IT
Leading us back to IT
For Divine collaboration
An exploration of Self
Means to healing ourselves
Reuniting with our Light, Power, and Authority
Understanding we are IT
Is the journey
While living Heaven on Earth

Our minds will label as "different"
Celebration of our differences
Is a celebration of our Union
With each other
With God
Period.

Relinquish Control

Relinquish control

Kindness for the soul

Relinquish control

Soothes your soul

Relinquish control

Heals your soul

Relinquish control

Is self_love don't you know?

Sitting in Silence

Sitting in silence
Preforms Miracles of Truth
As you get lost in quiet

Sitting in silence
Confirms with you
As you accustom to the quiet

Sitting in silence
Embraces the new YOU
As you accept the quiet

Sitting in silence
Provides answers for You
As you acknowledge the quiet

Sitting in silence
Expands for You
As you elevate with the quiet

Sitting in silence
Living within energy
As you transcend with the quiet

In Unity of Thyself

Love the Truth of who you are
As you embrace your woes
You will come to know
The Truth of who you are

Love the Truth of who you are
As you struggle to be you
You will understand
The magnificence of who you are

Love the Truth of who you are
As you heal the devastation from within
You will want to embrace
The magic of who you are

Love the Truth of who you are
As you discover the healing authority from within
You will want to seek more
The Divine essence of who you are

Love the Truth of who you are
As you become one with the Divine Love
You will wonder how you lived
The Unity with God is who you are

Letting Go

Letting go
Takes gumption
Presumption
Prescription

Letting go
Hard to do
Hanging on so hard
Cause that's what I do
Without reason
I still do

I find Faith
Cause I can not cry anymore!

I find Light, as I Believe
My Trust grows
Naturally,
Easily

Profoundly anchoring me
Within my SELF
I see my Light
Guided by it
I fly like an Eagle

Free flowing and beautiful
Grateful for my experience
My soul performs miracles
Transforming my circumstances

And I wonder,
Why was I hanging on so tight?
Afraid to let go?

Not anymore
"Bring it on" I say
My soul performs
Living Heaven on Earth
As God intends...

Rebirthing

Beautiful Soul
Obedient and free
Sparkling and Pure
Lovingly Graceful

Beautiful Soul
Travels with Grace
Purifying as you go
Connecting with Source

Beautiful Soul
Living humanly
To grow
Experiencing hardships

Beautiful Soul
Healing your trauma
Empowered as you overcome
Building Authority each time

Beautiful Soul
Stronger as you ascend
Transmuting what is yours
Producing deeper Gratitude

Beautiful Soul
Your forgiveness practices
Distinguishes forever
Guided by Pure LOVE

Always and Forever
Beautiful Soul
Latest eternally

Spiritual Journey

The *LOVE* in between isn't painful
Rather *painless*

The *LOVE* in between isn't painful
Rather *lessons*

The *LOVE* in between isn't painful
Rather *elevates*

The *LOVE* in between isn't painful
Rather *brightens*

The *LOVE* in between isn't painful
Rather *soulful*

The *LOVE* in between is *You*
The *LOVE* in between is *Divine*
Understanding this *unity* is the Journey

Sensory Observations

Sensory observations
Activates all parts of YOU

Seeing what you don't see

Hearing what you don't hear

Feeling what you don't feel

Saying what you don't say

Smelling what you don't smell

In YOUr awareness

YOU shall BE

Learning what it means
To be with YOU

Survivorship

It is not enough to just survive
As most people do
Encompassing the parts of them
Full of hurt and pain
To cope day to day
Temporary relief, sometimes
Not even aware
They are more than they know

More than they know
Is discovery of themselves
Required to live sustainably
Overturning ingrained beliefs
Beliefs, so deep not even aware they exist
But, are most powerful just the same
As people grip hard onto them
As if there is no other option
Keeping them in survivor mode
Deep pain still remains
Degrading themselves further still
Keeping up with dis-ease
Not even aware
They are more than they know

At some point people will realize
Through the Graces of God
They cannot continue in survivor mode
Simply surrendering
Releasing all they have been holding onto
Recognizing the mind cannot
Embrace their ill beliefs any longer
Their minds telling them
They "finally succumb" to the pain

But in reality,

They are surrendering to the
Greater part of them
The unknown part of them

The part that is in Loving Union
Spirt_God

Beginnings of refamiliarizing
Their truest essence
Their Authority within
Overturning ill beliefs
Exposing their True Way
Taking back their right
To live Heaven on Earth

This Journey begins
With profound sentiments
Loving themselves
Just even a little bit
Prevailing them
Into the Unknown parts of them
Revealing their Strength
Inherit within
To live Heaven on Earth

This Journey continues
As self_love grows
Exponentially, in fact
Through dedication and commitment
To Self
Loving kindness a byproduct
Always flourishing within
In unconceivable ways
Embedded in the Graces of God
Discovering within
Their Spirituality Birthed
A deeper awareness of
Soul_God
As they accustom to
Living Heaven on Earth

As their birthright…

Living Peace

I am Living Peace
As I venture out
Into a chaotic world
Sustainable within
Viable Strength within
My Presence igniting
A new world for me
As I live within me
I am profoundly loving as I do
As I BE in peace

As I Live in Peace
I am BEing ME
Practicing the Word of the Lord
Helping me to BE
Driving ME to BE
One with Thee
Inspiring ME to continue to BE
Upholding the Peace within ME

Assisting others to do the same
Cultivating their own relationship with
Spirituality, precious to them
Inspiring to Rise within
Meeting the Great Divine
As they learn to Live in Peace

As I Live in Peace
I know that I AM
BEing ME
As I need to BE
Transposing Divine Words on paper
For YOU to connect
With your Higher Selves
Re-uniting with the deeper parts of YOU
Conspiring to Elevate YOU
On this Earth
As you learn to take back YOUr Right
To live Heaven on Earth

Our Voices

We speak our Voices
To ourselves
To uncover our truth
Understanding its a requirement of Truth
Suppression only degrades us within
In ways our minds, does not know
Absorbed by our Essence
Transforming into physical hurt
Our minds will comprehend, eventually
Suppression is too great
Unbearable to hold

Acknowledging our Voices
Our minds release the hurt
Not caring what happens next
Our Essence has a chance
Finally!
Emerging for sustainable healing to begin

We speak our Voices
From our hearts, not from our minds
A place of vulnerability, our minds don't like to be
Fear may rise as we do, exposing is not what we do
Our minds will have us convinced
Living in fear all the while, normalcy so common
We are indifferent, so
Uncovering vulnerabilities are "new" fears, accentuating the normalcy
Unbearable to hold

Acknowledging our Voices
Our minds release the hurt
Not caring what happens next
Our Essence has a chance
Finally!
Emerging for sustainable healing to begin
Welcoming our Voices
Emerging our Truest form,
Our *Invisible Selves,*
within us all along,

Pure – Unharmed – Vibrant – Full of Divine Light
Understanding healing the unhealed parts of us
Means healing our minds' perceptions of old ways
Understanding what we are truly made up of
The magnificence of who we are
The brilliance of who we are
Holding innate wisdom
Always ready to steer our ships
A Compass of the Soul
Resembling the God within
Soul_God

Acknowledging our Voices
Our minds release the hurt
Not caring what happens next
Our Essence has a chance
Finally!
Emerging for sustainable healing to begin

Speaking our Voices,
Internal to us all
Unleashes the healthy parts of us
Emergence from the darkness
Transmuting of old ways
Our Souls knows what comes next
Integration with the Great Divine
Natural. Familiar.
A stronger version of US
Spawns a deeper desire
An addiction for sustainable happiness
Further exploration of Self is sought
As we learn how to take back our right
To live Heaven of Earth

BEcoming whole
Again. . .

Me

I jump up
I come down

I slide left
I slide right

I twirl then dance
I ponder with delight

I cry then laugh
With tight emotions inside

I flourish and expand
With purpose, I know

The presence inside
BEcoming ME
Is who I now know

Ignite YOUr Heart

The Power of the Soul
Resides within the awareness of the mind
Brought forward by the Sacred Heart
Only rising once explored
The Scope of YOU

Spirited by YOU, you are developing your spirituality. You are starting to venture into the unknown parts of you, looking for resolutions to your pain. As the single spark ignites a campfire, a dim flame on a candle just lit, or the one lever pull igniting a motor boat, you are preparing for takeoff into an unknown space that is YOU.

You are curious, afraid, and excited. You know you need something more and not knowing what it maybe. You are tired of the perpetual suffering in your life, day in and day out. You are lost outside of yourself, not understanding why you continue to live in pain. Deep guilt, fear, anger, frustration, shame, disappointment, and more continue to plague your life, and you don't know how you got here. Your body is failing you as a result of your tremendous stress. You wonder, "Is there a better way to cope with my life?"

Igniting your Heart is the exploration of YOU. It is a process in which you look into yourself for the answers you seek. Not knowing what you will find, you are ready with apprehension to explore a better way to live because, up until now, you haven't found a solution for *sustainable happiness*. It is a process of exploring and accepting what you find. It is a process dedicated by your efforts in exploratory ways to finding your TRUTH, your purpose on Earth, healing the unhealed parts of you buried in your subconscious, prevalent in your actions, and your mind has no understanding of why. It is the beginning of unleashing your internal Power, deep-rooted Authority illuminating YOUr LIGHT that is directional, grounding, and sustainable in your thoughts, words, and actions. It is the process of healing your body, improving your health in unconceivable ways, reducing perpetual stress, and improving the perspective of SELF, resulting in healthier relationships you keep.

Igniting your Heart starts with your free will - your free will to take action because up until now, nothing has been working for you. Your free will is the catalyst to your Forgiveness journey; without it, Forgiveness Healing cannot happen. You either want it or not. It is that simple.

FAITH of SELF

The Love for SELF
Prevails each time
In despair, I shall not be
Caressing the likes of ME
My Light shall BE
Forever and for always ME

The Love for SELF
Is more than I know
Below the surface
Deep into my Heart
Resides My God_Self
That will always BE ME

The Love of SELF
My Faith of SELF
Tested by circumstances
I call back my TRUTH!
Resembling My Love
Strength from within
My God_Self surfaces
Brighter than ever
Forever and for always for ME

The Love for SELF
The Greatest LOVE there is
In Union with the Divine
Moving mountains on my path
Remembering to Live in My Truth
Activating my God_Self in action and in reaction
Brighter than ever
Forever and for always
BEing in ME

Transpiring Hope onto Thee
I bring you ME
Describing the Essence of God

Activating YOUr will
To preform YOUr right

*Taking back YOUr right
To live Heaven on Earth*

Brighter than ever
Forever and for always bring YOU

Prescribe by the Divine within US ALL
From ME to YOU,
Namaste
With the deepest of LOVE

Divinely YOU

The Love for YOU
Is monumentally true

The Love for YOU
Is transpiring you

The Love for YOU
Is describing you

The Love for YOU
Loves you through and through

The Love for YOU
Is supporting you

The Love for YOU
Is Acquiring you

*The Love for YOU
Is Divinely YOU*

Discovery

Love the space you are in
As you express your Self

Love the space you are in
As you understand your Self

Love the space you are in
As you embody your Self

Love the space you are in
Regardless of the rising sentiments

Love the space you are in
Brings forward YOUr TRUTH

Love the space you are in
Because it is YOUr self_love discovery

Acknowledgement of the Soul

Free flowing and beautiful
No words can describe
The intense presence inside

Free flowing and beautiful
No sight can perceive
The magic residing within me

Free flowing and beautiful
The life rising within me

Free flowing and beautiful
The emerging Christ within me

Free flowing and beautiful
My soul is for me

A Prayer for YOUr Soul

Ignite the Soul within
As she travels the depths of your existence

Ignite your Soul from within
As a blooming flower that she is

Embrace your Soul from within
As the mind comes into alignment with Her

Embrace the rising Soul
For She is who YOU are
Existence from within
Holding profound Authority already within

Love the flourishing Soul
As you see Her brightness deep within
Holding Her Wisdom already from within

Sparking the mind's curiosity
As she rises
For there is deep healing transpiring

Accepting what is
Soothes the need for the mind's control

Trusting your Soul
As Divine Wings
Always guiding Her from within
Directional and purposeful
Without self-judgment

Bringing YOUr Soul into alignment
As the Divine Soul that SHE is

Free Will Activation

The mind adds complexity to our actions
Projecting perceptions that do not serve us
They never have, and yet
We persist within them
As if that is all there is

Unravelling the mind's perception
Is part of the Journey
To uncover our Truth
The Essence of who we are
Only buried from taught behaviour
It is up to us to choose

Do I want pain or Truth?

Do I stay here or see what's there?

Do I want to live this way?

Do I want to try happiness for a change?

Free will is YOUr agent for change
Without it
The same will be the same
Is that what you want?

Free Will opens YOU up
Infinite possibilities for YOU
Expressing the Purest of Love
Residing within YOU
Reuniting with ITs Peace
Re-familiar with ITs Stability
Reactivating with ITs Authority

Becoming YOU
BEcoming YOU

Free flowing and beautiful
Your Soul is to you

Your Soul Knows no Boundaries
When YOU BEcome YOU

Transcending into YOU

Transcending into *LOVE*
Requires forgiveness
A sense of letting go
Hardships removed
Opening up to the New YOU

Transcending into *GRACE*
Implements forgiveness
A sense of Authority
Growing YOUr Truth
Activating the new YOU

Transcending into *PEACE*
Accepts forgiveness
Opening YOU to receiving forgiveness
Exposing deeper parts of YOU
Embellishing the new YOU

Transcending into *YOU*
Understands the Depths of Forgiveness
Feels the impact of Spiritual Healing
Transmute suffering from your body and mind
Setting YOUr Spirit Free
Becoming familiar with Divine LOVE
Exposing deeper parts of YOU
Living in the new YOU

Beautiful YOU

Beautiful you
Free flowing and true

Beautiful you
Struggling to be you

Beautiful you
Healing to be you

Beautiful you
Loving to be true

Beautiful you
Transpiring to be you

Beautiful you
Winning the truth

Beautiful you
Is BEcoming YOU

Acceptance with Purpose

Lying here awake
Unable to sleep
As I explore the deeper parts of me
Curious with anticipation
I wait
Knowing I need to prevail

Within this life of mine
Looking for solace, layered in profound peace
Open with anticipation
I wait

Sitting in silence always preforms
Knowing the deeper parts of me
Will present its self
As it always does
Teaching me about me
I wait

Choosing to go deep within
Unexpecting what comes
I embrace what does
As this, too, is a part of me
Needing soulful attention
Healing my suffering means
Activating self_love unknown
Purifying my soul as I do
Acceptance with purpose
I wait

Profound gratitude
Surges through my systems with direction
Warming my body with infinite peace
Exciting my mind to new possibilities
My rising Soul emerges

Sitting in silence, I Be with my Soul
Embracing my awareness of Her
Appreciating my pain
Experiencing deeper Love I never knew

I wait

Free flowing and beautiful
I now know my Soul is to me

Beautiful Eyes

Beautiful eyes
Seeing what it sees
Brings me beautiful scenes

Beautiful eyes
So cleaver and clean
Brings me Light to be seen

Beautiful eyes
Transparent for me
Brings awareness for me

Beautiful eyes
Perceiving what I don't see
Brings enlightenment for me

Beautiful eyes...

Ahhhh, I see what YOU see
God before me

Beautiful eyes
Brings gratitude for me
Thank you for
BEing ME

Depths of Gratitude

Depths of Gratitude
Flourishes as YOU perceive
The *Life* within Thee

Depths of Gratitude
Enlivens as YOU activate
The *Light* within Thee

Depths of Gratitude
Moves you as YOU action
The *Authority* within Thee

Depths of Gratitude
Releases as YOU let it be
The *Truth* within Thee

Made of YOU

Expression of Love is infinitely guided

Expression of Love is sought remotely

Expression of Love is YOUrs to harbour

Expression of Love comes with benefits

Expression of Love transmutes the negative mind

Expression of Love unleashes the soul

Expression of Love heals the body

Expression of Love brings tranquility

Expression of Love is your existence

Expression of Love is made of YOU;

You are wrapped in Divine Essence

Reflective ME, Age 17

When I was young
Fear was always present
Harboured for safety
Unsure of me
My place in my world

When I was young
Insecure of me
As I cautiously experienced
Doubtful of what was
My place in my world

When I was young
I didn't like me
Unworthy of love
I degraded my being
Succumbed to my mind
My place in my world

When I was young
Not knowing what will come
My beautiful Essence
Built upon my experiences
Flourishing within God's Love
My NEW place in my world

When I was young
All that was
Prescribed by the Heavens
Learning the lessons
My Soul knows no boundaries
Beautiful and free flowing
My NEW place in my world

My young 17 self
Now knows Her Worth
Basketing is Pure Love
Acknowledging her Authority
That always was
In my NEW place in my world

Thanks Be to God

Self BEcoming

Expression of LOVE is delightful
As you BEcome familiar

Expression of LOVE is addictive
As you BEcome familiar

Expression of LOVE is without
As you BEcome familiar

Expression of LOVE is needed
As you BEcome familiar

Expression of LOVE is actionable
As you BEcome familiar

Expression of LOVE is valuable
As you adopt its familiarities

The Absence of Truth

The absence of truth
Is a wandering soul grasping at anything

The absence of truth
Leaves one untrue

The absence of truth
Is you without YOU

The absence of Truth
Is temporary if you choose

The absence of truth
Is a blessing of YOU

The acceptance of its absence
Is the journey to YOUr TRUTH

The acceptance of its absence
Holds deep healing for YOU

The acceptance of its absence
Is the only way to *YOU*

Scope of LOVE

As you be
Let it be

As you are
Bring it on

As you go
Let it go

As you come
Resemble what is

As you BE
Ignite YOUr Heart

As you BE
Embrace YOUr Awareness

As you BE
Embody YOUr Truth

As you will comprehend
YOUr Scope of LOVE residing within
Transpiring through all of life's circumstances
Finding the Grace of God as you do
Establishing YOUr specific dedication
A special BOND, a UNION
With the greatest part of YOU and
With the POWER to BE
An almighty source already within
Finding the God Presence
YOUr Soul already knows
Magnifies your relationship
Birthing your *Spirituality*
As your mind will call it
Unearthing new ways
To take back YOUr right
To live Heaven on Earth

The LOVE Beneath YOU

The Love beneath You
Rises up through you

The Love beneath You
Moves you

The Love beneath You
Comes for you

The LOVE beneath YOU
Triumphs because of you

The LOVE beneath YOU
Brings compassion to you

The LOVE beneath YOU
Knows what to do for you

The LOVE beneath YOU
Is part of YOU

The LOVE beneath YOU
Expands with the LOVE above YOU

The LOVE beneath YOU
IS in Union with the Divine YOU;
Fueling SELF_Love for you

Learning to Trust SELF

With each passing moment
Challenged by required lessons
Prescribed by the Heavens
I learn to Trust

Igniting my Awareness within
The Essence of my Trust for SELF
Resembles the Heavenly part of ME
Exercised through deep understanding of ME
I borrow from God's Graces
Instilled already within me
I begin to understand
What Trusting SELF really means to me

Trusting SELF requires absolutely NO self-judgement
Of any kind, that is expressed through thoughts, words, and actions
Knowing, if I do, consciously or not
I diminish my Essence of SELF Trust
God is teaching me to Live within my Essence
I begin to practice
BEing within the Whole of ME
In every moment of each circumstance
As hard as it may be,
My lessons are for me
Keeping me real within ME

Essence of Trust
Means you do not doubt
Means you accept without judgement
Means you are dedicated to SELF progression
Means you are kind to your SELF if you slip
For when you do
There is a deeper awareness of SELF
Rising to meet your mind
Revealing parts of you, wanting, needing
Healing of YOU, for the purpose
Of living Heaven on Earth

Essence of Trust
Is about cultivating Endurance
Ties to the Heavens above
The Center of Universal LOVE
We prevail as we do
In un_conceivable ways

We prevail!

Essence of Trust
Turns into Self_Love
Expressed through the Sacred Heart
Rising deep resolve sentiments of all kinds, transposing into
Lovable - Graceful - Peaceful - Foundational - Directional
Aspects of Self,
In all that we do, here on Earth
As we prevail into the Higher part of us
Identifying as our Higher Selves
Prevailing on Earth
As we live Heaven on Earth

Practicing how to Trust ourSELVES
Is Evolution
Living life on this Earth

Our Spiritual BEings
Already know
How to Trust SELF
Teaching the mind to follow, is the practice
Your Spiritual Journey
On this Earth

You are forever and for always
Guided by the Universe
Trusting in Thy SELF
As you receive...

Namaste

When Sadness Grows

When sadness grows
Let it be
It won't last forever
Unless you let it

When sadness grows
Healing is needed
It is your soul crying for help
Action it if you want to

When sadness grows
Dis-ease is activated
It is your body telling you
Your soul needs your help

When sadness is healed
Your soul is released
Free flowing and beautiful
Not anchored anymore

When sadness is healed
Your body responds
Reversing dis-ease
Mirroring your soul
Working together on Earth
With the purpose of
Living Heaven on Earth

When sadness is healed
Peacefulness sets in
Never to be erased
Fueling more healing to take place
Activating deeper Self_Love within

People I Love

People I love
Are teachers for me
As I learn to be Me

People I love
Are Saints to me
As I discover to be Me

People I love
Are God's love for me
As I transpire to be Me

People I love
Love me to be me
As I rise to be Me

People I love
Are here, so I can be Me
As I activate the Divine within Me

Choices

Inducing change comes
From changing actions
Free will is integral
Performing Miracles
Living Heaven on Earth

Rejecting what hurts
Fuels a deeper solution
For a better way
Filled with Self_Love
Living Heaven on Earth

Learning how to Forgive, gracefully
Struggling for its meaning at first
Applying the Law of Forgiveness
Opening up to a deeper perspective

Finally!

Discovering *YOU*
Liking what you find
Living Heaven on Earth

Practicing the New YOU
Identifying old ways
Deciding NO!
Preferring the New YOU
Always inviting the Divine YOU
Living Heaven on Earth

Celebrate YOUr Life

Celebrate the Life you have
Cause it is the one you have
Embrace all that you can from it
Profound learning will prevail
Bring you Heavenly perspectives
Solutions for circumstances in this Life

Celebrate the Life you are in
Dance to your favourite song
Releasing what is holding you back
Even if it is for a little
Ignite your Soulful Love
Embrace within it
It is Self_Love for you

Celebrate the Life You are in
Acknowledging your Worth within
Without shame, without judgement
The Purest of Self_Love rises
Recognizable to you as acceptance
Because you are dedicated to your happiness
Right here, right now
You are committed to your happiness
Performing Miracles on Earth
As an Expression of You

Celebrate the Miracles of Life
As you live your Life
Comprehending the Truth of who You are
Through mistakes experienced
All contribute to this wonderful Life
Leading you deeper into finding the True You

Celebrating your discovery of YOU
Brings you to infinite tears
Unable to physically hold it in
The Deepest of LOVE expression
A symbol of Spiritual growth
As you witness its effects

Transforming your Being in un_conceivable ways
Knowing you are living Heaven on Earth
Celebrating the Life you have

Just Because YOU Can

Eliminating disbelief of self
Requires one to truly understand
Their Scope of Self_Love
As they struggle to let go
Unfounded falsities of themselves
Revealing unknown parts of them

Just because you can
Found ability
Unknown to you
Fueling you
YOU then do it

Tired of the norm
Suffering unbearable
Desperate to ease the pain
Trying everything the mind suggests
Struggling to live a happy life
Forgotten what joy resembles
Set deep in their suffering
Forgotten who they are
Accepting "this" as is

Just because you can
Found ability
Unknown to you
Fueling you
Why not do it

But,
Their spirits not giving up
Using the body to communicate with the mind
Realizing there is another way
To live happily on Earth
The mind so tired it surrenders
Now, space for the spirit to rise
Slowly educating the mind and body
Of its existence

Just because you can
Found ability
Unknown to you, for now
Fueling you
To heal at an infinite level
Transmuting begins
Trying, knowing you can

Familiarity of YOU
Starts to reveal the truest essence of YOU
Marveling in your findings
Wanting more of the real YOU
Continuing with confidence
Powering through suffering
Accepting what was
Healing the mind
Freeing the soul
Uniting with God
One step at a time

Just because you can
Found ability
Now known to you
Fueling you
You will try
Again, and again

Because if you don't
You will never know
How magnificent YOU really are
Free from suffering
Hydrating with Divine Love
The deepest Love there is
Inconceivable to the mind
Healing YOUr body, and mind
Freeing YOUr Soul
Giving you foundational,
Sustainable Peace
Never knowing exactly

How You are:
Free flowing and beautiful
YOUr Soul is to YOU

Sacred Body

Your Body is Sacred
As she resembles YOU on the outside
Loving Truth

Your Body is Sacred
As she harbours YOUr untruths on the outside
Loving Truth

Your Body is Sacred
As she activates the mind's thoughts
Loving Truth

Your Body is Blessed
As she communicates with YOU
Loving Truth

Your Body is Blessed
As she grabs your attention for change
Loving Truth

Your Body is Blessed
As she facilitates the path to YOU
Loving Truth

Your Body is above all
YOU on the outside
Activating healing ways
For Loving TRUTH
As you become YOU

Welcoming YOU

As you Be
With you and me
Be with fourth sight

As you act
Within you
Be with thought

As you think
Outside of you
Be with compassion

As you recite
The goals for you
Be with God as you do

As you Become
Just let it be
The strength within you

As you transcend
Accept what comes
The authority within you

As you bloom into YOU
Welcome you
The understanding of the new YOU

Fun, Play, Laughter

Fun, Play, Laughter
Here to stay
As I learn to be me
Within the new version of ME

Fun, Play, Laughter
Found within me
From profound Healing of me
Igniting the best parts of ME

Fun, Play, Laughter
Has always been within me
Re_familiar sentiments rise
As I reunite with ME

Fun, Play, Laughter
Is my right to express
Confirming my beautiful Essence
Of what always was, is and will remain

Fun, Play, Laughter
Remedy in remembering ME
Reminding me of ME
All the infinite Healing I've acquired
The hard work remembered
Reconnecting to my Truest Essence
The Divine Presence of ME

Fun, Play, Laughter
Comes when I allow what is rising
As tough as it may appear
But never stronger than
My Authority within,
Because
I am Divine Essence
In Unity with God
Always connected
Never forgotten
Transcending
Heaven on Earth

Fun, Play, Laughter
My Purpose on Earth
Self-discovery of ME
Purest Love within
Activating MY Truth
As I learn to live
Within ME

Embrace YOUr Awareness

Self-Love achieved through means of Grace
Only realized through the Sacred Journey
Of layering back the suffering,
Revealing the True Self,
Healing the old you,
Adopting God's Truth as
YOU

Our purpose on this Earth is to heal what prevents us from living in complete Peace. Most of the time, we are unaware we are hurting ourselves, as we continue to harbour deep pain as if that's all there is. We continue to punish ourselves as we desperately long for peace. Happiness is rarely sustainable. Desperation and wonder set in, plaquing us further. When one chooses to explore their unknown parts, free will activates their understanding of what self_love means from a deeper perspective. Their Forgiveness healing journey requires perseverance and kindness directed back to self. Patience is born. Control is released slowly. Embracing awareness is not a destination but rather a journey, not linear but rather winding. As one starts to experience love for self, perspectives change, the body relaxes, and the spirit starts to unravel. Some level of peace sets in, gentle at first, then eventually, one resides within PEACE. The Love for Self activates your deeper Self. The Invisible Self steps forward in union with God for the sole purpose of transcendence through the Law of Forgiveness; this Holy practice is a means of purifying ourselves by shedding our untruths or false perspectives we hold tightly and, at the same time, empowering the Soul to rise steeped in resounding strength, power and authority. Life's greatest lessons are refamiliarizing ourselves with *TRUST, FAITH*, and *BELIEF* in ourselves and God. As we learn how to engage ourselves for the purpose of a better life, we can learn how to embrace our awareness of self through the Law of Forgiveness practice.

Embracing our awareness means we engage in union with the Higher Power and our deeper Selves to heal our misconceptions. When we learn how to engage ourselves, we naturally engage with LOVE and start to unravel the unknown parts of us, realizing our internal strength is supported by the Higher Source. Not only are we supported, IT fuels us. We are IT. As Energic BEings, we are individually connected to the Higher Source, a beautiful, free-flowing essence striving to live in finite ways on Earth. The Law of Forgiveness is a means of learning from our hurt, not being frozen with hurt but transmuting hurt so we can solidify our Essence and not degrade ourselves. Our Essence governs our thoughts, words and actions in everything we do without the hurt. This SELF governance is possible.

"Taking back our right" means we rise to meet our harboured selves while standing within our deeper Selves in unity with God; we suddenly stand within our LIGHT exercising the Law of Forgiveness. Each time we do, we activate deeper awareness of the Self, further cultivating our *Trust, Faith* and *Belief* of us. Since we are individually connected with God, this connection grows in girth, an unbreakable substance linking us to the Cords of Pure Love, Power and Authority. Enveloping this awareness each time you heal grows your Sacred Bond within yourselves. This Scared Bond anchors you for further exploration of you, transmuting fear as you practice the Law of Forgiveness. You are never alone; God works with you, facilitating the Law of Forgiveness Practice.

Birthing spirituality of you is this Sacred Bond. Living within this Sacred Bond means always living within your Light, providing you with resounding power and authority felt within your sacred heart. This magical place is never sourced from the mind. It is sourced from a place of peace and harmony of the sacred heart. Exercising your Light, Power, and Authority through the Law of Forgiveness empowers you to continue to live Heaven on Earth.

Silent Night

Embrace your soul
While you sit in silence, for the night

Embrace your soul,
For it is time

Embrace your soul
For the answers you seek are within
Your Wisdom

Your Wisdom is stored within your soul,
Profoundly guided by the Divine

Embrace Your soul and
Allow your Spirituality to
Activate your Truth
For your Truth lies with the Blessed Divine,
Intertwined - Co-mingled - Spearheading
Your Spirituality
Your Spirituality is your

Relationship with the Divine_YOUr soul;
Profoundly motivated for
Clarity - Transparency - Resolutions
You seek

Embrace YOUr soul

Embrace your soul,
For it will unleash the POWER
Already stored within
Your Essence

Embrace your soul
For the time has come
To sit in silence,
For a night

Embrace your Soul
The time has come
To take back your right
To live Heaven on Earth

Overcoming

There is nothing we can't overcome!
Spirited with profound *LIFE* within
We are commissioned to *BE*
Our presence inside,
Living Heaven on Earth,
Prescribed by the Lord above
As we overcome what is in front of us
Triumphing, our Truth prevailing
Each time we *Trust* ourselves
Each time we have *Faith* in ourselves
Each time we *Believe* in ourselves
Each time we choose, without regret to
BE YOU

As we overcome all that there seems to be
Uniting ourselves with the Lord above
In Union, most powerful absorbed
Embracing our magnificence
Learning we are GOD
There is nothing we can't overcome
The God within provides,
Stability founded in Infinite Love
Directional beyond the mind's capability
Trusting the God within,
Empowered to take on what seems to be
Knowing this too, shall pass
As you sit within YOUr Self,
The God within will prevail over you
Always within the direction, you need to be
Upholding YOUr greatest good, you shall BE
Where God deems you to BE
As you re-learn how to have:
Trust - Faith - Belief
Within YOUr Self_God, one and the same

YOUr Soul already knows
There is nothing you can't overcome

Sacred Bond

We are Divinely guided
Always going in the right direction
Flexibility,
Fluidity,
Resiliency,
Transparency,
Frequency,
Is LOVE
Embracing upon us

There is no resistancee
Strong enough
Preventing us from
Living in our Wholeness

There is a *Bond*
Profound enough to
Holding us together within ourselves
Capturing our Sacred Hearts
Propelling us In God's direction
For US

We are Divinely guided
Full of *GRACE*
Full of *MERCY*
Already
There is no Bond quite like
The Bond you already hold with God

For it is a *Special BOND*
Your Spirituality
A Sacred relationship between
Your *Soul_GOD*
One and the same
Emulating as the
Divine YOU

In the Shadows

You are in the shadows, NO more!
Belonging in the Light, is where you need to BE
Bright and Pure
Sparklingly with delight
Profoundly BEing YOU

In the shadows, is <u>not</u> a permanent place to be
Temporary only
To learn the lessons on Earth
Prescribed by the Heavens
Transcending, is your purpose
Learning how to take back your right
To live Heaven on Earth

In the shadows, is not scary
Dedication to YOU
Declaration of Trust
Pushing through the darkness
Acceptance of hurt
Requirement to enlightenment
Unravelling to get to YOU
Healing the unhealed parts of you
Triumphing prevails
Basking in lasting happiness
Is a celebration of YOU
As you shine brighter
Within YOU

In the shadows, an old part of you
Revealing itself for salvation
Bring forward untrue parts
Never part of your Truth of YOU
Realizing you are bigger than you knew
Facilitating inner courage
Driving you forward, to YOUr Self
The essence of YOU
Stronger than your pain
Commanding Authority founded in internal LOVE
Power embedded in SELF_LOVE

Functioning within the Light of God
Working from the Unified field
Burning God's Fire within

Coming to understand
BEing with the Power to BE
Is the only place where you want to BE
Where YOU are, right now
YOU_GOD

Is where the shadows, doesn't exist

My Worth is to ME

I am worthy, after all
Understanding all that was
Was as it was
Intentional with purpose
Exposing the TRUTH of who I Am

Worthy of so much than I knew
Believing the Scope of Me
Divinely powerful within my worth
I transcend as a result

Worthy of so much than I knew
My experiences of self-doubt
Fuels my deeper understanding of me
Celebrating the purest form of ME
Free flowing and beautiful,
As I am meant to BE

Deeper understanding of Me
Rises as I let it BE
The turbulence exposes what was of me
Solving the falsities of me
Trusting Divine guidance dedicated to me
Forgiving all aspects of doubt
Rejoining the Whole of Me
As I am meant to BE

I am worthy, after all!

Understanding of what is
Welcoming what's to come
As I practice the Whole of Me
Profoundly guided by the Forces of Heaven
Free flowing and beautiful,
My Soul is to ME

No Regrets

With no regrets,
I shall BE
Always drawn inside of me
Calm as I BE
Living the life
I'm required to live
Happy as can be
I am ME

With no regrets
Understanding my actions
Have led me here
Healing the unhealed parts of me
Celebrating my circumstances
Have made me stronger within

With no regrets
I continue to BE
Kind to myself
Embracing who I AM BEcoming
Open to what comes
Knowing I am getting stronger within
Making my Soul brighter still
Loving ME deeper still
I shall BE

With no regrets
I'm choosing
To BE
ME

Acceptance of the Rising YOU

Understanding your worth means
Understanding YOU
Free flowing and beautiful
Your Soul is to YOU

Capturing all there is of YOU
In every wakeful hour
Impressing upon the world

You are worthy!
You are worthy!

Believing YOUr worth
Stems from deep within
Building your Heart's strength
Perpetuating the God within
Enlivening YOUr truest Self
Activating YOUr purpose
Rising into your mind
Eliminating questioning of what is BEcoming

BEcoming the real YOU
No need for doubt
It is what it is
The beautiful YOU
Secure in the new YOU
Realizing the God Source within
Authority rising
Accepting the Gift
The life YOU are living
Free flowing and beautiful
YOUr Soul is to YOU

Blue Sky and the Sea

The bluest sky, calming sea
Your Beloved is upon thee
Swirling and becoming
Thoughtfulness and with purpose
Exposing YOUr Truth
Is upon you

The bluest sky, rippling sea
Turbulence is rising within thee
Anger surfaces without cause
Knowing it is yours without despair
You welcome it with
Purpose, Love and with Care

The bluest sky, glistening sea
YOUr heart expands, welcoming YOUr Truth
Transmuting untruths
Forgiveness with truth
Pure Love of truth
Exposing your truth
Settling in with your truth
Embodying your truth
Encapsulating God's truth
Resembling your truth
On this Earth
While living Heaven on Earth

The bluest sky, brightest sea
Your Beloved is upon thee
Always and forever
Igniting your *Internal Flame*
Bold and beautiful
Grows as YOU grow
Into the Light
Of Pure Love
Waiting for you
With an open embrace

Drifting White Clouds

The drifting white clouds
Calming and free
Rotating God's energy upon thee

The drifting white clouds
Bring solitude and peace
Circulating Love upon thee

The gloomy clouds are gone
Exposing truth in the storm's aftermath
Confirming YOUr resiliency
Affirming YOUr blessings
The truth of who YOU are
Surfacing to your consciousness
Bringing understanding
Fueling *Trust, Faith, Belief*
In the Divine above

The drifting white clouds
Is synonymous to personal growth
Preforming miracles
Sustaining and grounding
Embodying your newly found awareness
Carries you closer to YOU

The drifting white clouds
Loving you exponentially
Eternally set free
Your loving presence
Always Loved by
PURE LOVE
In unity with thee

Peeling Back Self-Doubt

I see my self-doubt
A deeper part of me
Floating around as if it belongs
Knowing it doesn't
Trying to understand it
I call my wounded self forward
With Love and compassion
I welcome this part of me
With caring Arms of LOVE

Seeing my self-doubt
Struggling before me
Uncomfortable with the Purest of LOVE
Present to capture
The Purest Love within me
Without judgement
I call forward the wounded part of me
Holding onto self-doubt buried within
Exposing the Truth of who I really am
I offer understanding to this part of me
With caring Arms of Compassion

Standing before myself
I feel the Divine Presence near
Encouraging me to face me
With open arms of empowerment
Fueling the deeper parts of me
Hosting Divine Love within me
I offer forgiveness to myself
Knowing it is time to do so
Realizing holding onto the false parts of me
Is not who I am, never was nor will it ever be
I offer my rising strength to my wounded self
With caring Arms of Authority

I watch as my Spirit releases my self-doubt
Myself is returning to ME
Empowered by my vision
Glee grows deep within
Wanting to complete my forgiveness
Deep within My Authority, I forgive
Forgive with understanding
Doesn't mean I condone the forgivable action
Means I choose myself
The purest parts of ME
Receiving Divine's loving forgiveness
For my unawareness of self-doubt
Prevailing into ME
With caring Arms of LOVE

Understanding now
My self-doubt really was perceived
Self-confidence of the lesser kind
Degrading my self-esteem to a higher degree

The Truth is
There is no need to control circumstances

I now know
Driven by the deeper parts of ME
Grounded in directional action
With a clear vision of ME
Sustained by my Authority within
There is no need to control!

Because,
I Do Not Fear Me

Rising Anger

I feel the resistance within me.
So strong. The anger rising, fast within me
Letting it out,
I say my words to myself
Knowing this is a part of me,
seeking healing of me
Not liking this feeling in me
I do not judge it. I allow it.
For the anger needs a voice only I can hear
Understanding this voice is the unhealed part of me
I choose to sit in silence. . .

Surrendering. . .

As I BE. . .

I BE. . .

I continue to BE. . .

Knowing, once I heal this part,

Reveals the brighter ME

Rainbow of Truth

Prism of Light
Spectrum of your Soul
Transparent and free flowing
Resembling the Spirit of Light
Resident of the Soul

Traveling Light
Illustrates the depths of ME
Layering my magnificence
Twilights and colourful
Growing aspects of ME
As I let it be
The beauty of ME

Spectrum of Light
Reveals the healing Soul
Accumulation of healed spirits of mine
From dark to light
From dull to bright
From bleak to warmth
Allowing me to unfold
Captures my Rainbow of Truth
The beauty of ME

Prism of Light
Journey to enlightenment
BEcoming one with God
Reflecting Source within
As Source Itself
One and the same
Living in finite ways
Purpose on this Earth
As we all,
Take back our right
To live Heaven on Earth

The love in between yourself
Transcends still
As you elevate further

Maturing beautifully
Achieving greatness as you BE
On your Earth you will see
The amount of Love
You will transpire onto many
Without thought or review
Knowing you are doing what needs to be done
You are touching many to do the same
As you have done, in this lifetime
Never doubt, as doubting is tempting
Bring yourself back to centre is the practice
I know you understand
The depths of your excellence
Will prevail you
In ways you don't know

Healing parts of you that still need healing
Will surface when it does
The deeper you go, the harder it hurts
Always knowing
I am with you, every step of the way
Getting through it provides confidence to the mind
A requirement as you ascend
Remember to always forgive yourself
The human you doesn't know what's transpiring and is
Learning to trust YOU
Learning to trust You_ME

Coming forward is your domain
Solace and free
You shall BE
An aspect of the beautiful ME
Choosing to be ME
We are magnificent beyond conception
Learning to trust, having faith and establishing belief
Is the journey
Within ourselves and in God
Because we are

Taking back our right
To live heaven on earth

Come forward
Coming forward
Came forward
You are not lonely anymore, not your truth

You are not worthless anymore, not your truth
You are not abandoned anymore, not your truth

You are safe
You are safe
You are made of the Light
This is your Truth; it always has and forever will be

Present before ME
I see myself needing much Love and Grace
She needs to find courage within the Light
Confronting her fears
Transmuting them
Taking back her LIGHT, POWER and AUTHORITY

In the magnificence of me
Standing up tall
Rooted in God's presence
I am taking back my right – shouting as I do

God's Intent for ME

God looking down at me
With delight
Sharing Divine Light
Makes me whole
As I prevail into ME

God present around me
Working with me
Supporting with intent
Taking me deeper within ME
As I prevail into ME

God within me
Tickling my awareness of Thee
Growing space within
Expanding as I connect
Embracing Divine healing energy
Enveloping around It
My Soul emerges
Free flowing and beautiful
As I prevail into ME

God inspires ME
To work with THEE
Never doubting
Always embracing
Exercising my right
In all life's circumstances
Practicing living in my wholeness

I AM, stable
I AM, grounded
I AM, compassionate
I AM, with purpose
I AM, in action and reaction
I AM, patient
Bring deep understanding, resolutions
As I prevail into ME

My God-Self emerges

Finally, within my consciousness
Perceiving the whole of me
Actively exercising my Right
Healing all parts of me
I know who I am
I know I can succeed

Within the Light of God,
I BE
Within God's timing
My soulful plan already determined by ME
Will present ITs self to the human me
Supported by Thee
I will know what to do
As my soul already knows
Teaching my mind and body
To perform as prescribed
I will continue for ME
Dedicated to ME
I will always prevail into ME

Free flowing and beautiful
My Soul is to ME

Healing Words from God

You are MY beloved
Stronger than you think
Find the strength within
To pull yourself through
For the Love of God is deep within
Never extinguished
Always lit
Driving you back to Grace
You can do this

Profoundly

You are able to pull through
Telling yourself: "Enough is Enough!"
Choosing the Light of God
As you are part of the Divine
And
All of humanity is supporting you towards Grace
Understanding your digressions will
Provide deeper insights into your journey
Back to yourself and God

Are you ready for change?

The Act of Forgiveness

The Act of Forgiveness requires a deeper understanding
It stems from letting go of control of the circumstance
It is founded within the Concept of Self_Love
Rooted within the deeper parts of YOU
Only attained if you allow yourself to explore
The unknown YOU

The Act of Forgiveness requires patience
As you practice letting go of control
Understanding, deeper insecurities will rise
Bringing the need to give yourself compassion
Bringing the need to confirm your dedication to you
Providing yourself permission to allow
Remembering, no self-judgement now
As you explore, the unknown parts of YOU

The Act of Forgiveness engages YOUr breath
Facilitating deeper breathing
As you practice letting go of control
Realizing YOU are in control
As the unknown parts of you rise before YOU
Releasing the tension through tears
Your body accepts the breath, as it is YOU
Breathing deeper still, as you recognize
The Depths of You,
The invisible part of YOU

The Act of Forgiveness lead by the Essence of YOU
Engages with the Higher Power to BE
YOU are immediately filled with ITs Healing Energies
YOU see clearly now the circumstances before you
You accept responsibility of your digressions
You apply the Law of Forgiveness
Understanding 'they' are acting out of fear
You forgive 'them', with understanding from a higher level
You forgive 'them',
As you work through the unknown parts of YOU

The Law of Forgiveness proceeds deeper still
As you ask the HIGHER POWER TO BE for forgiveness
Of the digressions you have made
Understanding why you have, from the unknown parts of you
You do not apply judgement to the Law of Forgiveness
Felt deep within YOUr essence
YOU are truly forgiving
The HIGHER POWER TO BE forgives
YOU immediately drop to your knees
Humbled now, forgiving YOUr Self
From a place within, filled with LOVE
Deep levels of gratitude born
As you work through the unknown parts of YOU

Experiencing the Affects of Forgiveness
Like never before
Your body responds kindly
To the Energy of Gratitude
Brought to you by YOUr Essence and
The HIGHER POWER TO BE
A part of you, deeper still
Working in union as IT has always been
Understanding the unknown parts of YOU
Fuels deeper acts of Self_Love
As you have now discovered the unknown part of YOU
Working for YOU
Holding your best interest, always
Caressing you in every circumstance

Remembering to breathe in
Activates the next forgiveness act of *SELF_LOVE*
As you continue exploring the unknown parts of YOU

The Warrioress

Among us all
Exists the Warrioress
Built for combat
Built for nurturing
Exists within ALL of us
As we explore the tender parts of us

The Warrioress
Combative in nature
Preforming powerful notions
Executing tremendous loyalty
Protecting the ones She loves
Understanding Her Truth
Prevails through
Every time She steps up
For Her Self
As she explores the tender parts of her

The Warrioress
Also knows deep down
Her true nature
Is not to fight but to protect
She transmutes hurt into Light
Spirited by the Great Divine
Always within
She executes Divine Authority
She executes Divine Power
Emulating Divine Light
She is loyal to herself
As she explores the gentle parts of her

The Warrioress
Holds significant parts
Defining Her existence
On this Earthy Plain
As she prevails Spiritually
She honours and respects
Her experiences on Her journey
Of self-discovery

Vital to Her existence
She cannot be ignored
For if she does,
She is denying parts of Her

The Warrioress
Doesn't control
Rather sets free

The Warrioress
Doesn't anticipate
Rather allows

The Warrioress
Embraces the softer sides of Her
As she balances
Between Divine Energies
Embedded in her Truth
Divine Feminine and
Divine Masculine Energies
Loving all aspects of Her
Knowing her Divine guidance
Is to BE
On this earthy plain
As she takes back Her Right
To live Heaven on Earth

Taking Back MY Right

Understanding the Truth of who I AM
Embraces all parts of who I AM
The wounded self
The healed Self
Combined with the Holy Spirit
I AM taking back MY right

When my wounded self rises
She rises with ill sentiments too
Wanting to heal her
To stop the pain
To release her from
The hurt and pain there is
Because the Love for my SELF
Because the Love of God
I AM taking back MY right

There is only one way
Unleashing the unhealed parts of ME
Accepting this is temporary
I welcome the hurt
Empowered,
Guided,
I confront my pain
The ugliness presents itself
Knowing I AM prevailing
In this moment of transcendence
I AM taking back MY right
Knowing these sentiments are separate

From my spirit
I prevail
Necessary, I know
I take back all MY power
I take back all MY authority
I gave you spirit of hurt!
You are not my truth!
I command you to GET OUT!
In this moment of transcendence

I AM taking back MY right

My spirit looks weak at first
Nourishing her is next
As I apply forgiveness to all parties
Understanding how I have strayed
From my Divine path,
Away from my purest of TRUTH
Leading back to God as needed
I AM taking back MY right

Laws of forgiveness applied
Necessary for spiritual healing
Removing the karmic cords
I forgive those that hurt me
I ask for forgiveness from the Almighty
I forgive myself for my thoughts, words, actions
Stemming from the deeper parts of ME,
Self_Love never experienced before,
And is somehow very familiar
I AM taking back MY right

Fulfilling my earthly purpose
I took back my right
To live Heaven on Earth
Bringing me back to familiarity
Coming home,

I am ME,

I am ME,

Stronger each time
To do this again and again
Committed to Loving my SELF
Committed to finding MY way back
To the Divine ME

To My Wounded Self

You stand before me
In need of some help
Enduring hurt to the nth degree
Not knowing what to do
Simply beside yourself
Holding onto youthful circumstances
Harbouring the hurt as if it is security
As you always do
And where has it taken you?

Harbouring these ill sentiments
Degrading us deeper still
The time has come
To deal with this now
It is time to choose

Thank you for bring this forward
I am dedicated to our growth
God Loves you profoundly
Resentment and jealously is not our truth
Aren't you tired living with this?
It is time to choose the Light

I am dedicated to our growth
Going deep to unleashing this hurt
Learning it wasn't the source
Of what was really hurting you
I forgive; As I do to repairing you
Fortifying in God's Healing Energy
Revealing our Loving Truth

I see your Halo now
Pure Love is now you
Colliding with the rest of ME
You are back home again
Free flowing and Beautiful
Our SOUL is to ME

Praising Actions of Within

During tough times, trying times
Love yourself more!
Continuing to thrive is necessary
Persevering through feelings of despair
As you continue to live your human experience

During tough times, trying times
Deep love within will carry you through
Into the next profound learning of YOU
Designed to prevail each time
Only if you allow it

During tough times, trying times
Understanding, despair is temporary
Once you face it and take it on
Applying forgiveness is required
You then, end it permanently

During tough times, trying times
Bring life back into you
Experiencing, even this shall pass
Beautiful Essence rising
Bringing understanding of what was
Bringing acceptance of what is
Gratitude floods your system
Praising the Divine within
Building authority within
Acknowledging the stamina within,
To do it all over again.

Worthy of Forgiveness

Forgiveness is confusing for some
Exploring the Depths of Thee
A necessary action to exercise
Solving the unhealed parts of us
Making sense eventually
The mind catches up
Revealing the Purest Essences of Thee
Forgiveness is necessary

Worthy of Forgiveness
For you and me
We accept the concept
A necessary action to practice
Through Acceptance comes Understanding, then
Letting go depths of your pain
We are accustoming to carrying
Without reason, we just do
We practice the
Law of Forgiveness

Activating forgiveness is not a mental exercise
It can never be! Our minds are not equipped
Forgiveness stems from the Heart, always
Like anchoring ROOTS of the Tallest Tree
Forgiveness is born in a magical place
Only accessed through YOUr Soul
Already residing within your Spiritual Heart
Waiting for Thee to access
Unleashing lasting happiness,
Peace, that is YOU

Applying forgiveness is as natural
As our bodies needing food and water
Deserving of YOUr Love
You are to Thee
Setting you free, finally
Working through suffering
Breaking through to YOU
Deserving of YOUr forgiveness

Is your right to apply
So, you can *live Heaven on Earth*

Worthy of forgiveness
Means applying value to YOU
Deserving of YOUr value
Placing great emphasis
Deeming you are important to YOU
An expression
ROOTED IN SELF_LOVE
Only YOUr Soul can activate
Attributing to Divine Love
Fueling YOUr soul to deliver
Through the Law of Forgiveness
For Thee

YOU are
Worthy of
YOUr Forgiveness

YOU, In The Present Moment

Loving the space, you are in
From the most magical place within
Steeped with Pure Love and Grace
Holds deep Authority within
As YOU practice the present moment
Freeing YOUr Self of worry and doubt
Understanding to remain within your essence
It is required to adopt YOUr Self in unfamiliar ways
Letting go of hopeful sentiments embedded in doubt
Letting go of fearful sentiments embedded in insecurities
For truly living within your essence holds the deepest of TRUST
Trust holds confidence in the not knowing
Trust accepts with confidence, what will be will be
This is what it means to live in the present moment

In reality, circumstances will be what they will be
It is up to us to accept God's Will
Without judgement nor the need to control
Control is based in fear, often confused with hope

Sentiments of hope
Embedded with anticipation and doubt
Of a desired outcome
Isn't living in the moment
Fear, a separate sentiment
Driving anticipation of the mind's desired outcome
Isn't living in your Truth

The Love you cultivated for SELF
Sits in the center of your being
Guiding YOU
Comforting YOU
Driving YOU
Hope isn't needed
Fear isn't present
For in this present moment
YOU are with SELF
Immersed in PURE LOVE
Known as the unknown

Discovered as the Great Divine, ITself
LOVING YOU unconditionally
Passionately
Favourably
Directionally
Safely
Where you need to be
At any giving moment

Accepting the present moment
Accepts YOU
Accepts God
Accepts the not knowing
Accepts the safety attributed from your growth
Accepts the calming presence within
Accepts the Truth it represents

Living in the present moment
Does not activate anticipation
Does not entertain fear
It activates the internal breath
Inviting SELF to remain in Authority
Inviting SELF to remain in the LIGHT
Reminding SELF of ITs Power
In union with the Great Divine
Practicing lessons learned
Remaining true
Stabilizing essence now known
As YOU

Parts of ME

Just being in the despair of me
Working with the unhealed part of me
Without judgement
I just...allow
Tears flow uncontrollably now
I know I am healing

Crying so hard as I sit in my discomfort
Knowing it is the unhealed part of me
My mind feeding me unkind
I allow to get to the root of ME
Giving my unhealed part of me a chance
To reveal what's on her mind
Giving her this moment is
Acceptance of what is

Knowing what this is
My path to healing me
It is always about healing ME
My response to the outside
The effects of the outside on ME
Unraveling the trigger is about ME
Healing is always about ME, not the outside
I still LOVE the outside
Teaching me
As I am BEcoming ME

In this moment, I choose too always BE
In my Wholeness, forever and always
Flipping over to the True ME
I choose not to get lost in the outside
Coming back to centre, clearing my mind
Dissolving old perceptions of me
Choosing my healthier path
My soul continues to sing
The songs of freedom
As I continue to
Live Heaven on Earth

Imparting YOU

Imparting *knowledge*
Requires *experience to be had*
Flourishing as you age gracefully

Imparting *wisdom*
Requires *deeper understanding*
Attributing solitude on your path

Imparting *Love*
Requires *Self_Love of YOU*
Embodying the Essence of You

Imparting *Gratitude*
Requires *Appreciation of YOU*
Relating you to everything

Imparting *Truth*
Requires deeper *Scope of You*
Practicing Divine lessons learned

Spirited You

Spirited you
So heightened and true
BEcoming you is what you do

Spirited you
BEcoming and true
Releases what isn't you

Spirited you
Worthy and true
Actions what is you

Spirited you
So safe and true
Grounding what is you

Spirited you
Loving and true
Enlivens the *Essence of YOU*
Welcoming the bigger part of YOU

Tremendous Degree of Peace

Tremendous Degree of Peace
I feel as I heal
My body melts into my seat

Tremendous Degree of Peace
I embody Divine healing energies
Transforming my weak body

Tremendous Degree of Peace
My deep heart swells with gratitude
My body releases tears of joy

Tremendous Degree of Peace
My soul grows stronger and stronger
My mind diminishes even more

Tremendous Degree of Peace
Like nothing I've known before
Transcending over me
Elevating me to new heights
So, I can learn to BE ME,
Again

Healing Sounds of Summer

Early morning reflection on a beautiful summer day
No other human around
Only Mother Earth's Loving sounds
I sit in my *Tree of Life*
Propelled to communicate
With Her comforting Earthy energies
Solidifying my Authority within
As I enjoy BEing with ME

I hear Canadian Geese squawking as they approach me
I hear Mourning Doves signing beside me
I hear Crows cawing with each other, on the left of me
Reflecting on how Nature interacts
Understanding there is no separation
Between ME_Nature

I hear the Winds moving the trees' canopies
Brings physical and mental calmness
As I step forward from myself

I feel the blissful Winds caressing my skin
The warming Sun on my skin
Brightening my face
Illuminating my new perspectives of ME
Loving the space I am in

Cool humid air brings wakefulness of the day
Pulling my attention inwards
Reflecting on my human life
Celebrating my spiritual journey
Recognizing how much I have changed
BEcoming a better version of mySELF
Not wanting it any other way
Loving the space I am in

Appreciating all the vibrant colours my garden offers
Building on the diversity around me
Loving what God has created
Understanding I am one with all of IT
Grounding sentiments rises

Anchored to Mother Earth
So, I can fulfill my human journey
As my purpose prescribes
While sitting in my,
Tree of Life

Never taking for granted
What life has to offer
In the simplest of forms
Lies the Energy of Christ
In the single atom
Full of Loving Energy
We are made up of IT
Along with the Earthly Elements
Also made up of IT
Makes us all the same
Loving the space I am in

Sounds of Summer
Magical in all elements
Reminder of what we are
More than we know
Vibrant
Clear
Free flowing
Beautiful
Connected
Until we do know,
Expanding our awareness,
Dedication of Trust,
Expression of Love,
Appreciation grounded in Gratitude,
Building upon Faith and Belief still
We are God
Divinely Perfect in every way

Living Your Humanness on this Earth

Profound sentiments of LOVE rise
As you comprehend your unknown-ness,
The invisible parts of you
Collaborating on your behalf
As you live your humanness on this Earth

Tears surface as you uncover more of you
Understanding the stemming cause
Unleashing parts of you
Transcending into the unknown parts of you,
As your awareness grows,
As you heal the unhealed parts of you,
You blossom into a glistening butterfly
As you live your humanness on this Earth

Colours so bright
Seen by your spiritual eyes
Beyond everything your human eyes have ever seen
Mesmerized by this vision
You are in complete trust
You are rooted in deep peace
Stabilized like never felt before on this Earth
You know,
You are transcending
In this magnificent moment
You are in the presence of God
You never want this to end

Instantly,
Gratitude floods your system
Feeling God's blessing energy
Healing your dis_eased body
Taking over your physical body
As you receive this LOVING energy
You receive with purpose
Gently allowing the Universal LOVE
Into your body
Uniting your spirit with IT
Prevailing as you do
Accepting in complete trust
You receive with delight

As you live your humanness on this Earth

Loving yourself more because,
Witnessing the miracles of the Divine in action
Experiencing the miracles of the Divine's LOVE for you
Adopting the miracles of the Divine's ways
Learning the finite ways to live
Mirroring the LIGHT before you
BEcomes your purpose on this Earth
Profoundly grounded as you do
Directional as IT provides you
Stabilizing you
You proceed with Divine LOVE
In all that you do
In every moment
As you live your humanness on this Earth

You are committed to YOUr Self
Wanting to regain your familiarity
Of your unknown parts of you
Establishing a deeper connection with the LIGHT
BEcoming closer to the Divine Essence
Founded within
Surfacing the deep Self_Love
You are excited to have found
As you practice living your humanness on this Earth

This dynamic is called your spirituality
Exclusively YOU
As you BEcome familiar with YOU
Cultivating YOUr relationship with GOD
Uniting the two
As you practice living your humanness on this Earth

Recognizing your purpose
You are taking back YOUr right
To live Heaven on Earth
As you practice living your humanness on this Earth

Embody yOUr Truth

In my wholeness
I shall BE
Forever and for always
As the Divine ME
In finite Union
As I live
Heaven on Earth

Exploring your Truth is a compilation of gradual changes as you exercise life through your Heart. *Igniting YOUr Truth, Embracing YOUr Awareness* of your Truth is all about finding YOU and healing misconceptions of YOU through the Law of Forgiveness. *Embodying YOUr Truth* is about living within your Holiness. Learning from a cellular level, YOU are GOD - one and the same – YOU are not separated from IT. Instead, you are IT, working in collaboration for the greater good of YOU. Embodying is not a mental exercise, for the mind has no concept of your Holiness and God. As your Holy Self steps forward, all parts of you will learn how to live or come into alignment within your Holiness. This is what embodying is all about - transitioning into your Holiness in every action and reaction as you live your human life on Earth. It is YOUr Holiness who governs all of you!

As you explore the deeper parts of you, your mind catches up with your Truth. Slowly. Progressively. Understanding the parts of you, the roles they action and the value you place on these parts is the awareness you are seeking. As you heal your suffering, your Truth (YOU) will rise. The undeniable Authority and Power IT holds takes over naturally. Recognizing this shift is the embodying exercise requiring self-dedication to a life of practice. BEcoming into YOU even further is implementing life within your Truth as YOU. This transition is the state of learning "how" to live and BE within the NEW YOU. It is the by-product of fortifying your deep residence of *TRUST, FAITH* and *BELIEF of YOU* and, therefore, *GOD*.

Embodiment is a fundamental shift that happens when you decide to live within your Truth and not the mind's programming. The speed at which this shift unfolds depends partly on your free will. Your free will always plays a big part in your spiritual maturity. As free will is exercised, the resistance within you subsides long enough to remain open for what comes next, and your Truth will rise as you do your Forgiveness healing work.

Embodiment is a loving place to BE. Always be kind to yourself and free from judgment. You will witness *Heaven on Earth* by allowing your Holiness to be front and centre. Circumstances will fall into place without thought. Joy and Gratitude fill you at a cellular level, uncontainable at times, and your body releases LOVE with excitement. Profound Peace is a permanent resident within you. By choice now, you work at remaining within this state because it is a much happier place to live, achieving sustainable JOY.

Sacred Living is what I call this state.

Calling Back My Truth

I stand before you
In the depths of ME
I call back my Truth from thee

The LOVE I have for me
Is the bigger part of me
Transcends all negativity of me
Understanding my headache is temporary
I call back my Truth from the unhealed part of me

Choosing not to stay within this pain
Activates resounding self_love
Preparing me
To unfold the unhealed parts of me
Calling back my truth
Is what I need to do, NOW

Embracing this special part of me
The healing energies within
Brings calming sentiments
Familiar sentiments
Enveloping the stronger parts of me
My rising soul always preforms
Within my authority and self_trust
Foundational in action
Directional in reaction
Hosted by the larger Divine I know
My Soul embraces the larger Divine,
again
In union,
to take back my Truth

I am prevailing
As prescribed by the Heavens
Forgiving the unhealed parts of me
Thanking myself for the experience
Sending gratitude
As I fill myself with the Power to BE
I am prevailing

Into ME

Stronger still…

Perceptions of YOUr Truth
Is God's Truth
As you transcend on this Earth
You will continue to grow
Within the Light of God
As intended for all reading this poem

Achievable to those
Willing to transcend themselves
The parts holding them back:
Anchoring themselves within lies and deceit
The sentiments causing misperceptions of self
Those are not yours to keep, Child of Mine
Understanding your Truth
Requires deeper scope of Self
Until you learn the lesson
Lessons will continue to prevail you

Accept the true you
Means you accept YOU

Accept the Truth of YOU
Means you Love YOU

Taking back YOUr courage
Means you reside within YOUr Power
Means you reside within YOUr Authority

Calling back YOUr Light
Means living within the stronger parts of you
Means accepting the God within as YOU
Means NEVER falling back into old perceptions
Means practicing living Heaven on Earth

As you take back the right
To live heaven on Earth
You are transcending
Into the God within YOU

Grounding for Life Pays off in Dividends

Grounding for life
Anchors your soul
Untouched by circumstances
Dedication to the work
Pays off in dividends

Grounding for life
Takes work of dedication to YOU
Takes inner stamina to preserver
Takes self_love without judgement
Pays off in dividends

Grounding for life
Means living Heaven on Earth
Means accepting vulnerabilities
Means applying the law of forgiveness
Means connecting with Divine healing energies
Means finding your essence along the way
Pays off in dividends

Grounding for life
Results in stability
Results in clear direction
Results in knowing what actions to take
Results in knowing what actions not to take
Results in free-flowing ways
Results in letting go expectations
Results in fundamental trust
Pays of in dividends

Grounding for life
Anchors your soul
Preforming miracles on Earth
Untouched by circumstances
Healed weaknesses within
Dedicating to the work
Living a blissful life
Acknowledging you are living Heaven on Earth
Paid off in dividends

Flow

Profound LOVE
Resident of your soul
Loves you very much
As you are
Allowing the Graces of God
Flow through you
Activates your truth
Always

The FLOW is intense
Beautiful and free
Moving lovingly through out
Leaving you with

Peace

Self_Compassion

Self_love

A sense of what is right, for you
Actions needing to be actioned
Powerful direction
Authority within
To BE YOU

The FLOW never leaves you
Always present within
Never absent
Waiting for activation, from YOU
Enlightenment for you
Realizing the power IT holds for YOU

Easily accessible
You come to know
Building trust as YOU do
Naturally, Faith and Belief
Transcends into YOU
Each time you activate
The FLOW

As the wind flows through the trees
Caressing the anchoring tree
Lightening up ITs magnificent presence
The Flow anchors YOU

The Graces of God
Resembles the FLOW
Within YOU
Understanding the FLOW
Is YOU
Always in Union
With God
Formulating Divine One
YOU_GOD
Most powerful understanding
Most authority living
Within this Flow
You will want to remain
Right here
Within IT

The Flow

A State of BEing

I look into my mirror
What do I see?
I see YOU staring back at Me
All loving as can BE

Looking in my mirror
A true reflection of Me
Brilliant Me, I see!
As I BE

I like looking into my mirror
For a deeper understanding of Me
As I grow further into Me
Reflecting back at Me
As I BE

Looking in a mirror was hard for me
Not understanding the essence of me
Defrauding me was all I knew
As I wasn't BE

Now I know
As I continue to grow
I look into my mirror
And like what I see
For all my life's experiences
Formed me
As I BE

As I BE
Is the goal to be
A state of BEing
Longing to want to BE
Practicing to remain in BE
Always and forever
In union with the
Divine_ME

Creating a NEW Life For You

Elevating with the energies around you
Transcending because of your truth
Exhibiting the magnificence of you

Acquiring the love around you
Takes deep understanding of you
Exhibiting the magnificence of you

Accustoming with what is
Takes Faith, Trust and Belief
Actioning the Energy within

Forth coming and true
Your essence will BE
Practicing the world of within

Loving and YOU
Delighting of you
Creating a new life for you

Expiring Thoughts

Expiring thoughts let out steam

Expiring thoughts are blessings. You will see!

Expiring thoughts bring awareness of what was

Expiring thoughts bring understanding of what is

Expiring thoughts rise with acceptance

Expiring thoughts are surrendered with ease

Expiring thoughts are always forgiven

Expiring thoughts are the old version of you;

Exposing the TRUTH of who you are;

Living Heaven on Earth with Divine Intention

I'm Not Afraid

I'm not afraid
Of what's inside
Hurting me intensely

I'm not afraid
Of what I don't understand
Knowing what's to BE

I'm not afraid
Of the person inside
Healing parts of me

I'm not afraid
As ITs foreign inside
Loving essence of mine

I'm not afraid
Of what's to BE
Unleashing the God in me

I'm not afraid
As I BEcome ME

I'm not afraid
Newly found depths of ME

I am no longer afraid
Of ME

Mirror, Mirror on the Wall

Liking what you see
Is judgment free
Rising sentiments of glee

Liking what you see
Inviting YOU forward
Finally appreciating what you see
Uncovering a version of you
Free from hurt
As I live Heaven on Earth

My Story of Truth

My Story of Truth
Reveals in many ways
Exposing my vulnerabilities along the way

My Story of Truth
Unravels in other ways
Learning the depths of my soul

My Story of Truth
Forgives the untruths held
Healing the physical parts of me

My Story of Truth
Allows me to flourish
Dancing triumphantly, All of Me

My Story of Truth
Welcomes me as ME
Acting Divinely for eternity

Regaining Yourself

Right here right now
I am here
With me
And with God
Breathing in The Light
Regaining my Peace
Feeling Calm reclaim by body
Rejoicing to find ME again
Remaining within this moment

Hope keeps me in the future
Fear keeps me in the past
The breath keeps me in the present

Right here, right now
I am here
With me
And with God
I shall remain with ME

Control keeps me frozen in time
Anticipation keeps me in the future
My awareness keeps me breathing

Right here, right now
I am here
With me
And with God
I shall remain in my Authority

This moment shall pass
As I practice God's lessons I've learned
Always remaining within
Focusing on my body's tall tales
Understanding that I am human
Learning my life's circumstances
Bring me closer to ME
A deeper understanding of ME
Prevailing into ME

I shall remain in the present
Surrendering control

In God's timing,
All will be as it needs to BE

Divine Feminine Energy within Everyone

Understanding YOUr truth
Requires a deeper perspective
Of the unknown parts of YOU
As you continue to prevail
You must come to know
All parts of you
That make up YOU

As you prevail
Revealing YOU
You recognize, the softer part of you
Delicate with powerful LOVE for Self
You accept the Divine Feminine present
Within your Soul
Energy you cannot live without

Rising of the Divine Feminine Energy
Implicit to nothing you know
Exploring deep sentiments of
Trust, Faith and Belief
Within YOU, cultivating fluidity of Self
Birthing the likes of YOU
Finding deep rooted self_compassion
Nurturing abilities exploding
Applying to Self as requiring
Always hydrating the Soul
Rebuilding YOUr Truth as you do

Overcoming internal weaknesses
Embedded perspectives of the old
Never selfish
Never in self-punishment
Softness breeding confidence
Softness breeding internal Power
Softness breeding internal Authority
When nourishing YOUr Soul
Through the Law of Forgiveness
Standing within YOUr LIGHT
As you live your life on Earth

Never apologizing for YOUr softness
Rather celebrating IT

Never shameful of YOUr softness
Rather exercising IT

Never supressing YOUr softness
Rather letting IT out

Never excusing YOUr softness
Rather standing within IT

Never dismissing YOUr Softness
Rather accepting all of IT

Never ignoring YOUr Softness
Rather balancing IT

Strength and Stamina birthed
Through adopting YOUr softness
For your softness
Nurtures YOU,
LOVES YOU,
Resulting in a
Balanced YOU

Adopting the softer part of YOU
The nurturing part of YOU
Enhances your performance on Earth
As you balance YOUr softness
With the Divine Masculine Energies
Fostering the Whole of YOU
As you practice how to
Balance YOU,
all of YOU
Is your journey
For taking back YOUr right
To live Heaven on Earth

Riding the Wings of Change

I once felt scared of change
Bring forward muscle tightness
Mind unclear of my future

I once felt doubtful of me
Bring forward fears in my head
Preventing me to seeing my way

I once felt the crippling effects
My thoughts brought on for me
Struggling to be me

Now, I know more than I knew
The love within me is something new
Enveloping me inside out

Now, I know my loving self
As my strongest self
Transcending to be ME

Now, I know my Holy Self
The Truest Essence of mySelf
Resembling the Divine ITself

Now, I know I am traveling
On my Wings of change
Living Heaven on Earth

I Shall Prevail

I turn to you Heavenly Father
Asking for forgiveness
As I have strayed from Thee
Choosing the wrong aspects of me
I now know my way
The Light of God is my path
Embracing all of you
I shall prevail

Enduring the lessons of life
I understand Thee
Deep within, You shall BE
I find YOU there
Collaborating with me
As you have always been
Embracing YOU
I shall prevail

Touching the depths of my heart
I find YOU there
Caressing and soothing me
Forever and for always
YOU shall be within me
Embracing YOU as you are
Teaching me my new ways
Elevating my awareness of Thee
Embodying YOU in finite ways
I shall prevail

Uniting with Thee
Bringing profound knowledge of me
Deep in the depths of my soul
I now know
I am YOU, and
YOU are ME
Together we are invincible
Producing miracles on this Earth
Deepening my grounding roots
You have giving me

Embodying YOU in finite ways

I am prevailing before YOU
With Your Grace
I am prevailing into YOU
As YOU intend
Free flowing and beautiful
My soul is to ME

Gift of Life

Exploring the truth of who you are
Is an expression of trust, in yourself
Wondering how to proceed through
Deep despair within, riddled with fear
Preventing progress forward

Exploring the truth of who you are
Is an exercise of trust, in yourself
As you find your strength
Through your breath
Calming the body, then the mind
Understanding fear is part of you
But. It. Is. Not! Who. You. Are.

Exploring the truth of who you are
Is a practice of trust, in yourself
Realizing 'fear' is a part of you that is not your truth
Getting to the root of the fear
Makes it clear to the mind
The reasons for the fear
Unraveling to reveal YOU

Exploring the truth of who you are
Is a celebration of trust, in yourself
Applying forgiveness from the heart
Brings you closer to God
The purest of LOVE
Forever healing you
Revealing the truest form of you
In union with the Divine presence
YOUr truest form of you is set free

Again,

Again and,

Again

On This Earthy Plain

Rooted in life
Like an anchoring tree
Solid as can be
Preforming miracles for ME
Sustainable in all things
As I stand tall
In my life to BE

Rooted in life
Foundational like the tallest building
I do not bend
I gently sway to the blowing wind
Reminding me
Of my place in Heaven
In my life to BE

In my life to BE
On my earthly venture
I understand my true Purpose is to BE
Capturing the Essence of Me
Uniting with the Holist of ME
Representing THE Holy Divine
As sustainable as can BE
I practice to BE
In my New Essence of ME
On this Earthly Plain
In my life I am BEing

As I am BEing on Earth
Understanding what is real, what is not
I keep grounded in perspective
That I am ME first
Human second.
Living gracefully,

As I BE
On this Earth
Propels me
Evolving as I should

Sacredly
Lovingly
As I BE on this Earth

Rooted in this life
I know I will BE
As I need to BE
Learning the Sacred parts of Me
Empowering ME
Enveloping ME
Within the Sacred parts of ME
Uniting with the Higher Source
I will always BE
Practicing BEing ME

Most at Peace

In the silence
My words will be
Comforting to me
As I learn to be ME

In the silence
The world subsided long enough
To hear ME
Telling me words of comfort
Formulating the likes of ME
Blissful,
Magical,
Beautiful ME
As I learn to be ME

In the silence
I am most at peace
Judgement doesn't exist
As I travel through the mist
Uniting with the Grandeur parts of ME
Celebrating all of ME
I am ME
There is no other place to BE

In the silence
With,
ME

Ego's Transformation

The ego plays a role
Vital to our growth
Acceptance of it
Opens Heaven's door
To your soul
Leading you to
YOU_GOD

The process of healing
Changing the mind's old ways
Does a number on the mind
Surrendering, is part of it
Replacing old ways with
Finite ways
Resembling the God within
Living Heaven on Earth

The ego's job is to just believe
Believe in itself,
In YOUr spirit,
In The Holy Spirit,
In the Unity of the Divine One,
YOU_God above all

The ego's role becomes smaller, and smaller still
Always trying to go back to old ways
Our Unity outweighs in:
Strength,
Stamina,
Endurance,
Authority,
Peace,

Sustainable Peace, is undeniable
Even the ego will agree
Life long commitment to SELF
To living Heaven on Earth

Expression of YOU

Expression of Truth
Inspires you to be YOU

Expression of Truth
Engages YOU

Expression of Truth
Loves you to be true

Expression of Truth
Requires you to be YOU

Expression of Truth
Brings you, YOU

Expression of YOU
Loves to be YOU

The Mother In Me

The young Mother in me
Anxiously waiting
My birthing miracles
That are etched in my mind
Honoured to have them
To do the best that I can

Nurturing and caring
Raising my young
Not knowing what will come
Deep healing of me
Triggered by my young
The child within me
Needing to be free
From self-hate and self-sabotage
The untruths parts of me
Dissolved through forgiveness
Guidance from within

My deep Motherly Love
Still exists, only deeper still
The adult me Loves my child self
My inner child is one with my SELF
Free flowing and beautiful
As she needs to BE

Profoundly Loving my young
Observing my young grow into them SELVES
Giving them space
Expanding within
Learning the lessons of fate
Within their Divine Selves

I remain the Loving Mother that I am
Now living within a NEW space
The truest of Pure Love
I encapsulate within my BEing
I am me

I AM ME.

Exercising YOUr Right

Life's triggers will always remain
It is about your response to them
Counts the most
In your spiritual healing
Of Thee
Life's triggers will always remain

Searching for fuel for the pain
That once was
Recharging what is gone
Forth sight and BEcoming
Takes precedence
Of Thee

Life's triggers will come at you
Celebration of YOUr Truth
Activating YOUr new ways
Acknowledging what you have BEcome
Choosing not to go back

Loving YOU,
Takes *Trust of Thee*

Life's triggers will come at you
Practicing being in your new BEing
Prevailing as God intends
Accepting what comes
Sitting in silence
Dedicated in healing YOU
Taking back the right
As you have learned

Loving YOU,
Takes *Faith of Thee*

Life's triggers will come at you
Acceptance of what is
Always going within
Verifying YOUr Truth
Connecting with the Divine

For direction, reprieve
Exercising your right
To live Heaven on Earth

Loving YOU,
Takes *Belief of Thee*

Always...

Free flowing and beautiful
My Soul is to ME

I Love My Son

I love my son
Like the brightest sun
Beaming deep warmth

I love my son
In the truest form
Activating deep wisdom

I love my son
In the simplest ways
Professing true ways

I love my son
Learning deep ways
Building stronger ways

I love my son
Watching him succeed
In his ways

I love my son
Profoundly ME
In my ways to BE

I love my son
Thanking ME
As I BE

My Soulmate

I do not accept
Your lies and deceit

I do not accept
Your hurt inside me

I do not live
Your Truth within me

I do not take on
What is not mine

I know your Truth is within
As I see your Light from within

Your kindness is Truth
As it grows deeper within

Your Love is recognizable
For the Love of God is within

You will learn
How to live within Him
As you take back your right
To live Heaven on Earth

The Love between Us

The love between me and you
Is yet to be seen
As we beam
Beyond our galaxy
Fulling our dreams
With love between me and you

I hold you in my heart
When we are apart
For you are part of me
Holding me in your heart

The love between us
Is yet to be seen
As we BE

Between us, we are love
As God intended
"I Thee Wed", God said
Holding us together
Intertwined in this life time and others to come

Forever and always,
I will LOVE You
Thank you for being you

Those you Love

Responding to those you love
Those that need you the most
Those that love you the most
Those in your Soul Group
Those requiring your attention
Are those in your life for a reason

Responding to those you love
Have hidden Treasures of Scope
Unraveling parts of YOU
Deeper than you know
Are soulful aspects of you
Yarning to be with you

Responding to those you love
All the joyful moments and
Those unpleasant moments
All bring attention to your awareness
So, you see, your responses of Thee
Requires deeper understanding of YOU
Leading to the unhealed parts of you
Your Soul is yarning to be with YOU

Responding to those you love
Miraculously improves from patience
Sparking deep rooted compassion
As you implement deep Spiritual Healing
Knowing it is the ultimate in Self_Love action
Bringing on your Truest Self
Celebrating the new YOU
Your Soul now joined with YOU

The Love for My Children

The Love for my children
Moves me every time
Holding tight in my heart

The Love for my children
Teaches me every time
Understanding of my Truths

The Love for my children
Binds me to new ways
Activating deeper Love within

The Love for my children
Causes for celebration
Purifying my Essence within

The Love for my children
Continues to grow
Unleashing New parts of ME

The Love for my children
Purposefully crafted
Revealing what is about ME

The Love for my children
Deep gratitude grows
Embodying my New ways

The Love for my children
Sourced deep within
The best parts of ME
The healed parts of ME
Resembling my Divine SELF

The Love for my children
Representing,
The LOVE for my SELF

Trusting

Trust as you grow because,

Trust ignites

Trust fulfills

Trust fuels, what is to BE

Trust is authoritative

Trust comforts

Trust preforms

Trust explores

Trust ignites the LOVE in your heart
That is,
YOU!

The Power To BE

Bright colourful flowers growing with love
Glistening birds flying gracefully around
Authority trees standing tall
Deep green grass lush as can be
Walking through the Garden of Heaven
Recognizing what I have BEcome
The Magnificence BEing that I AM

Just skimming the yellow pathway as I move forward
Light on my feet, feeling with all of my senses
Absorbing the surrounding vibration
My BEing present with ME
I see before me the Greater part of ME
Waiting patiently for me, as grand as SHE can BE
Beauty, I have never seen
Taking my hand to see the Power to BE
Uniting me with an even deeper part of ME

Gasping with glee
I fall to my knees
Crying uncontrollably
Experiencing deeper loving emotions
Words cannot come close
Expressing blissfully where I am
Remembering where I came from
Knowing. I. AM. HOME.
Overwhelming to see the Power to BE
Always loving ME

Understanding the Power to BE
Is deep within ME, the Fire within
Igniting my Sacred Heart, I now
Embrace all of ME, as I practice
Embodying all of ME

I now know,
Free flowing and beautiful
My Soul is to ME

Loving YOUr Self Through and Through

Living in the present moment
There is no hope
There is no fear
There is only trust

Living in the present moment
There is no doubt
There is no insecurity
There is only trust

Living in the present moment
There is no future thinking
There is no past hurt
There is only trust

Living in the present moment
There is no wishing
There is no present hurt
There is only trust

Living in the present moment
You are trusting the unknown part of you
You are trusting the Great Divine
You are confident in YOUr Self
You are confident in not knowing
You are confident with acceptance
In this present moment
Transmuting if needed
Transpiring as required
Loving as you BE

In this present moment
With BEing YOU

Earthly Elements

As I BE
Breathing into the Scope of ME
Surrounded by Divine Love
Seeing beauty all around me
Witnessing Divine magnificence
I acknowledge how far I have come
Appreciating my hard work
Dedication to ME
Uniting with the bigger part of ME
I understand the subtilities
Of Divine's communication
With Me

I receive ITs messages
Through the Earthly elements:

Whispering:
"All is where it needs to be"
I receive.

"You are stable within"
I receive.

"I know where you are
Within YOUr presence
Deep within
I am here for YOU,
Holding YOU,
Soothing YOU,
Directing YOU,
Guiding YOU,
LOVING YOU"
I receive.

Gentle breeze on a humid day
Reminds me
The fluidity of my Soul
Reminds me to Be:
Without control
Without anticipation

Without worry
In the present moment
With ME_God

The warmth hugs my body
As if to say:
"I got YOU"
"You are safe with ME"
I receive.

As I sit accepting all of this
I feel the Sun's rays
Funneling through
The Tree's canopy
Directly onto ME
Highlighting the place where I sit
Confirming my understanding
Of God's messages for ME

Deep seeded emotions
Rise to my human eyes
Unable to contain
The Love inside
Expelling God's TRUTH
In physical tears
Cleansing my spiritual eyes
My third eye re-balancing
Readjusting back to the True ME

I am whole again
As I practice
BEing with ME
In complete
Unity with God
Always…

Viable Strength

Viable strength
Derived from the Soul
Fueled by the Divine
Captured by your Sacred Heart
You are BE

Viable strength
Never from the mind
Always from the unknown
Collaborating with higher parts of YOU
God leading you
Teaching you
Captured by your Sacred Heart
You are BE

Viable strength
Grows through practicing
Lessons learned
Sparked by your infinite healing
Fueling deep gratitude
Loving YOU even more
You are BE

Viable strength
Isn't about being strong
It is about being BALANCED
Divine Feminine Energies with
Divine Masculine Energies
Found within YOU
Forming aspects of YOU
Adopting their presence
Understanding their worth
Brightening your Soul
Balancing between these loving energies
Attaining stabilizing strength
Prevailing you still
You are BE

Viable strength
Based in foundational PEACE
Never in self-compromise
Never in self-judgement
Never in shame
Never in aggression
Never in fear
Always from Eternal LOVE
As you live IN FINITE ways
You will forever BE

Thanks be to God

Thankful

Thankful for my experiences
Now that I'm healing
I see my suffering as an asset
Brings understanding and Truth
My BEing prevails
Encapsulating Divine Light

Spectrum of Your Soul

Prism of Light
Spectrum of your Soul
Transparent and free flowing
Resembling The Spirit of Light
Resident of the Soul

Traveling Light
Illustrates the Depths of ME
Layering my magnificence
Twilights and colourful
Growing aspects of ME
As I let it be
The beauty of ME

Spectrum of Light
Reveals the healing Soul
Accumulation of healed spirits of mine
From dark to light
From dull to bright
From bleak to warmth
Allowing me to unfold
Captures my Rainbow of Truth
The beauty of ME

The Prism of Light
Journey to enlightenment
BEcoming one with God
Reflecting Source within
As Source Itself
One and the same
Living in finite ways
Purpose on this Earth
As we all,
Take back our right
To live Heaven on Earth

The LOVE in between yourself
Transpires still
As you elevate further

Maturing beautifully
Achieving Greatness as You BE
On your Earth, you will see
The amount of Love
You will transpire onto many
Without thought or review
Knowing you are doing what needs to be done
You are touching many to do the same
As you have done, in this lifetime
Never doubt, as doubting is tempting
Bring yourself Back to Centre is the practice
I know you understand
The Depths of YOUr Excellence
Will prevail you
In ways you don't know

Healing parts of you that still need healing
Will surface, when it does
The deeper you go, the harder it hurts
Always knowing
I AM with YOU every step of the way
Getting through it provides confidence to the mind
A requirement as you ascend
Remember always to forgive yourself
The human you doesn't know what's transpiring, and
Learning to trust YOU_ME

Coming forward is your domain
Solace and free
You shall be
An aspect of the beautiful ME
Choosing to BE ME
We are magnificence beyond conception
Learning to TRUST, having FAITH and establishing BELIEF
Is the journey
Within ourselves and in God
Because we are
Taking back our right

To live heaven on earth

Come forward
Coming forward
Came forward

You are not lonely anymore, not your truth
You are not worthless anymore, not your truth
You are not abandoned anymore, not your truth

You are safe
You are safe
You are made of The Light
This is your Truth; it always has and forever will BE

Present before ME
I see myself needing much Love and Grace
She needs to find courage within The Light
Confronting her fears
Transmuting them
Taking Back Her LIGHT, POWER, and AUTHORITY

In the magnificence of ME
Standing up tall
Rooted in God's Presence
I take back my rights – shouting as I do! . . .

Practicing the Lessons

I am a Spirit of God
Residing within ME
Profoundly good
Clarity beyond conception
I prevail beyond me
In search of Thee

Understanding beyond the Scope of me
Revery of Thee
Takes courage beyond belief
Developing deeper sense of belief
Belief of Thee prevailing onto me
Is Faith of Thee
Is Trust of Thee
As common as the breath I take
Thee profoundly within ME
Magnificent beyond feeling as I know it
Drawing within a deeper sense of ME

Feeling the burning fire within
Rising within, fury full of resounding LOVE
I prevail onto Thee
I humbly accept Thee
I humbly forgive Me
I humbly embody
The whole of ME and
I BE

Practicing the lessons of Thee
Brings me to my knees
As I prevail onto Thee
Privileged for this
Dedicated to Thee
Means I am in complete state of Self_Love
Resembling Thee in all that I do,
In action and in reaction,
Within all of life's circumstances
I will always remain with THEE

Living Heaven on Earth
As a free flowing and beautiful BEing
As a humble servant of THEE
As an enlightened human being
I will always remain with THEE

Tree of Life

The Loving Source within
Activates a Life within
Attributing to Divine ways
Blossoming in unknown ways
Knowingly, it is the way
Adopting these ways
As I grow within
My Tree of Life

Tree of Life
Resembles a New way of Life
Practicing in finite ways
New behaviors blossoming
Attributing to profound infinite healing
Bringing back to Earth

Living my Journey
In conjunction with my Earthly Family
Transpiring still...
Bringing forward profound ways
Known to ME
Explicitly moving, to the nth degree
I am living within
My Holy Self

Tree of Life
Represents spirituality
The connection between Self_Divine
A *Bond* solidly holding onto
The greatest part of YOU
The Sacred YOU

As you live in this new way
Non-breakable, that you are
As long as you stay within
This *Bond of Life*
Living within this Unity
Propelling you naturally
Effortlessly

Sustainably

The Tree of Life
Continues to grow, beautifully
Through the body
Upwards, meeting the Heavens
Downwards, anchoring to Mother Earth
Outwards, expanding in girth
Perpetuating the constant
Etheric connection with intense Divine Love
You are living in BE

With rising sentiments
Tears of gratitude
Fills your human body
Expelling God's Truth
Leaving behind
Profound peace
Calmness at a cellular level
You are BEing

As God intends for ALL
To take back our right
To live Heaven on Earth
Residing within our Holy Selves,
In *complete* union with God

Continuance—
The Evolution Never Ends

Your Reality

Love the space you are in
As you *Aspire to new heights*

Love the space you are in
As you *Recognize yourself*

Love the space you are in
As you *Elevate your Truth*

Love the space you are in
For your *Truth is all there is*

Rejoicing Love

Profound Love resides within
Not like any love you know
Deep within
Foundational like no other
Loving you unconditionally
Brings you new ways
Of BEing with YOU

Directional Love resides within
Bringing Essence of Trust
Like trusting your best friend
Without questioning
Just knowing this friend will always have your back
You Trust unconditionally YOU

Prescribing Love resides within
Capturing your confidence, courage and
Your LOVE for SELF
Utilizing the Light of God
Shining bright from within
Moving mountains on your path
Exploring your ways
In unconventional ways
Bringing the NEW you to YOU
To BE YOU

Accepting LOVE resides within
Where IT has always been
Deep within
Transpiring a knowing
Unraveling a familiarity
Preferring IT as a result
To BE you within Divine LOVE
Accepting the NEW you to be YOU
Without doubt
As IT has always been, but forgotten
Reclaiming your right
To live Heaven on Earth

Rejoicing LOVE resides within
Understanding your journey
Celebrating your lessons
Flourishing because of your growth
You ponder what was, as you give thanks!
Deciding never to go back
Empowered to persevere your path
Dedicated to the cause of YOU
Accepting YOUr Authority along the way
Living within your purpose
You are deserving of YOU
Living your Truth
Free flowing and beautiful
YOU now know
YOUr soul is to you!!

Sustainable YOU

Connection to movement
Any kind of movement
Brings unity within
Unity with speed producing movement
Unity with water movement, side to side, forwards backwards
May bring uncertainty as movement requires *Trust of Thee*
Movement, the mind cannot bare, not knowing what it will bring
The mind resisting, counter movement, moving against the forces of movement
A reaction common to the mind
Unsustainable to YOU

Connection to movement
Any kind of movement
Ignites the Spirit to flow freely, naturally, patiently
There is no resistance to the movement upon thee
Acceptance of movement brings stability
Groundedness within the present moment
Revealing YOU as you do, the parts resisting you
Understanding these parts of you needing attention of you
Facilitating deeper growth
Peeling back the old you as you do

Breathing in the Light of God
Provides direction for YOU
Unraveling the untruths of you
Uniting you with the bigger part of YOU
Your mind starts to recognize what you are doing
Embracing your Light, Power and Authority of YOU
Activates the Light of God within you
Growing within this sacred space
You feel yourself grow within
Resembling your Tree of Life
Spirituality resembling deep connection to the other side
This connection is your sustainability within
Your Godly Truth within
As you take back your right
To live Heaven on Earth
Time and time again…

Nature_ME

Sitting on the edge of the dock,
Listening to all the sounds of Mother Earth
Her Earthly elements speaking to you through your observatory senses
Brings profound calmness; every cell relaxed, your mind is finally empty
Your spirit comes forward dancing to the sounds, free-flowing and beautiful
The warmth of the Sun, glistening on the water,
Animals communicate instinctively,
Bright blue sky with white fluffy clouds floating by
Your eyes are mesmerized by the vast shades of green all around,
In the distance across the lake, your eyes rest on ITs sights lost in no thoughts

You just BE

Your spirit connects to the Spirit of God found in all the Earthly Elements
Unknown in the moment, your mind simply surrenders to Mother's Green Earth
In that moment, your spirit familiar with ITs surrounding
Realizing YOU are home
Comfort, security, resiliency rises as your spirit rejuvenates
To live Heaven on this Earth

I am ME

Round and round I go
Up and down, I come
Running from here to there
Seeing the world without a care
Loving the Truth for ME
Embracing the LOVE of ME
Expelling my Truth before thee

I am ME

I AM ME

The Truth of NOW

What is,
Is

What isn't,
was

What will be,
It doesn't matter

What is now,
Is all there is

The Progression of YOU

The Power to BE
Is the Journey to enlightenment
Lighting up the path to YOU
To BE
Is BEing that
As you are BEcoming that
Both a noun and a verb
At the same time, distinguishing between
As you travel on your spiritual Journey
As you grow into YOU
In Union with God
Practicing new ways
Living in the Divine space
Your Holy Self emerges
As you now
BE
the NEW YOU

Understanding

I love you a great deal
You are part of me
I'm sorry for intruding
I care about your feelings
You are important to me
We are a team
Experiencing different things
Things that have hurt us in different ways
Both ways are valid
Birthing patience and acceptance
Of our circumstances
We will get through it together
We always do
We are stronger together
Fueled by our love for the other.

I love you profoundly
More than I can put into words

Words from God to You

God standing before ME
Bright as can BE
Talking directly to ME
Instructing ME to write this:

Beloved Child of Mine
Honoured and freed
Allowing what is true
To be revealed as needed
Performing Miracles of Life
Living Heaven on Earth

Beloved child of mine
Free-flowing and beautiful
Allowing sentiments of Joy
Rise, above all else felt
Acknowledging your Truth
Is the mission
Performing Miracles on Earth
Living Heaven on Earth

Beloved Child of Mine
So true, as YOU
Injecting the Essence of Love
Into what you do
Living Heaven on Earth

Beloved Child of Mine
Comprised of Purest Love
Travelling the World
Basketing in my Glory as you do
Teaching others to do the same
Living Heaven on Earth

Beloved Child of Mine
Example to many
Humbling experience
Expressing my Truth as you do
Performing Miracles on Earth
Capturing the hearts of many

Illustrating it can be done
Living Heaven on Earth

Taking back the right
To live Heaven on Earth
Is the purpose
As all will see, eventually
As you did
My Beloved Child of Mine

YOU_GOD

Miracles of Life
Birthed within us
When we came to this Earth
Prosperous and full of Vitality
We are here
To celebrate US

Celebration of Life
Brings understanding of
Our true calling
To BE ourselves
In the purest sense
Past the hurt and pain
We agreed to experience before we arrived
Forgetting our truest sense when we arrived
We prevail towards ourselves while we are here
Was the plan along
The coming to BE
The BEcoming
Is the practice
The Journey
The enlightenment way
Of discovering
Embracing
Embodying
Living in our Truths
As prescribed by
YOU_GOD

Harmony of Life
Transcendence of YOU
In collaboration of the Great Divine
Producing YOUr Holy Self
One and the same
Beautiful like you've never known
Holding the Graces of God
Deep within YOU
As you live your life

Maneuvering through circumstances
In complete Authority and Light
Blissfully accomplishing your goals
Productivity without fear
Productivity without shame
Productivity without guilt
Productivity without worthlessness
Productivity <u>with</u> Direction
Productivity <u>with</u> Stability
Productivity <u>with</u> Sustainability
Productivity <u>with</u> Groundedness
While living within
YOU_God

The Divine would Say. . .

Possessing PURE LOVE
Takes gumption
As you set out to explore your Truth

Possessing PURE LOVE
Takes tenacity
As you BEcome into you

Possessing PURE LOVE
Takes self-compassion
As you give yourself understanding

Possessing PURE LOVE
Is required of you
As you struggle to be you

Possessing PURE LOVE
Is simple as one, two, three
As you release control of you

Possessing PURE LOVE
Is magical to the mind
As you re-familiar with you

Possessing PURE LOVE
Is available to you
As you open up to YOU

Smile Till It Hurts

Smile till it hurts
Cause it is what to do

Smile till it hurts
Cause it is easy to do

Smile till it hurts
Cause it is required to do

Smile till it hurts
Cause it is healing as you do

Smile till it hurts
Cause it is satisfying as you do

Smile till it hurts
Cause it is loving YOU as you do

Mountain_Ocean

Where the Mountain meets the Ocean
Land and water cohabit brilliantly
Projecting beautiful sentiments onto its spectators
Capturing our Essence as we observe
Sharing feelings of grandeur
Moveability and stability attributes
Found within us
Reminders of our Truth
Actioning efforts while planted firmly within our Right
Prevailing as the Mountain and Ocean before us
We are one and the same,
Energic presence united in a Sacred Bond
Only realized when one resides within Divine Love
Recognizing Divine Love within the brilliance before us
Forever grateful
Where the Mountain meets the Ocean

Within ME

In my Wholeness, I shall remain
Celebration of ME
Conspiring to BE
SOUL_GOD
As required to BE
Loving ME
Always and forever
ME

The Love I feel
Within ME
Around ME
Is from ME

Beautiful sentiments
Building Joyous thoughts, words, actions
Respecting what I have BEcome
Understanding the depths of my Soul
Fuels my appreciation
Finding my infinite understanding
In all things around me
Giving thanks each time
Builds MY resiliency
A significant part of ME
Hosting the other parts of ME
In celebration of what I've BEcome
Exercising my Right
To live Heaven on Earth

My beautiful Soul is to ME
Now that I honour
The depths of *MY SOUL*

In my Wholeness, I shall remain
Now I know,
There is no other place
I'd rather BE than
Within ME

A New Day

Today is a New Day
To practice again
Fortifying YOUr Truth
With each attempt at
BEing YOU

Today isn't yesterday
It will never be
In this moment, you are safe
In this moment, you are required
To BE
Within YOUrself
The safest place to BE

As you practice again
Fortifying YOUr Truth
With each attempt at
BEing YOU

Today is a new beginning
Clean slate at discovering
The profound Essence YOU are
Prescribed by the Heavens
Unravelling the Whole of YOU

As you practice again
Fortifying YOUr Truth
With each attempt at
BEing YOU

Today is a new understanding
Celebration of your mistakes
Providing the greatest reveal of YOU
Never self-sabotage again
Never self-judgement, was what it was
Always in Self_Love for a change
Embracing the scope of YOU

As you practice again
Fortifying YOUr Truth

With each attempt at
BEing YOU

Tomorrow is another New Day
We will not worry about
Enjoying today too much to care
Knowing you will prevail tomorrow
Living in unified
Trust_Faith_Belief
YOU_God

Tomorrow is tomorrow's reveal
Learning what it is when you do
Timing when you are ready to learn
A deeper part of you still
In this present moment
Remaining within

As you practice again
Fortifying YOUr Truth
With each attempt at
BEing YOU

On a Rainy Day

I look outside on a rainy day

I see the beauty of ITs day

The vivid colours of ITs way

I see its resemblance in a way

Compelling me to give thanks

As ITs vibrant Essence makes ITs way

Exposing the Earth in a magnificent way

Bring forward a familiarity with ITs way

Understanding ITs Truth is looking for you

Earthly Essence is prevailing you

Encompassing ITs Truth is a way

To build Unity within the Divine You

Our Community

I am Love
You are Love
They are Love
We are Love

Knowing we are connected
Interconnected
Fondly connected
Profoundly connected
Makes us all the same

We are different
Outside only
On the surface
Uniquely packaged
Makes us all attractive

We are energy
Waves of Bright Light
Free flowing and beautiful
Magnificent beyond conception
Keeps us connected

We are Divine BEings
Living a human experience
Taking back the right
To live Heaven on Earth

Holding Kindness for Another

Hold kindness in YOUr Heart
For you and me

Hold kindness in YOUr Heart
As you see

Hold kindness in YOUr Heart
As an element of compassion for me

Hold kindness in YOUr Heart
As I struggle to be me

Hold kindness in YOUr Heart
Cause it is loving support for me

Hold kindness in YOUr Heart
As I grow to BE ME

Your Tribe

Your Tribe prevails you
Always in your best interest
Even though you may not be aware
Know, you are in the Tribe you are in
Working together in this lifetime
In other lifetimes still
Adhering to your Heavenly plan

Already prescribe
By the Divine Presence
Inside YOU

Your Tribe stays with you
As you mature spiritually
In the cycles of time
Learning from each other
From good circumstances and in bad
But, always with the:
Highest Good Intention
Deepest of Love shared between
Purpose of transcending
Guidance from the Great Divine
BEcoming brighter

Already prescribed
By the Divine presence
Inside YOU

Your Tribe is never mistaken
Consists of blood relatives and not
People who you get along with and not
Acquaintances of brief interactions and longer
Even strangers passing by, sharing brief glances
People you loath, especially these folks
Everyone you come into contact with, for whatever reason
Belongs to your Tribe
Your Spirit Family
Each Loving YOU
Dedicated to helping YOU

Spiritual maturity
An evolution of YOU

Already prescribed
By the Divine presence
Inside YOU

Your Tribe is your blessing
There is so much mutual:
Respect – Honour – Integrity – Compassion – LOVE, and more
In the Tribe, held by all members
Helping YOU learn the hard lessons
So, you can evolve into God's image
Learning how to take back your right
To live Heaven on Earth

Already prescribed
By the Divine presence
Inside YOU

You are Called

I Trust THEE
To guide ME
Where I need to BE
Revealing parts of ME
Paying attention to ME
Trusting in ME
Without fear of ME
Breathing into ME
Experiencing all of ME
Holy Self leading ME
Is living Heaven on Earth

Rise up,
To Be
What you are here to BE
The best version of YOU
On this Earth
Experiencing this life, you have chosen
Purifying YOUr Soul, is the task at hand
Always with patience
No judgment at all
Self_Love carrying you through
Divine supporting YOU
Forever BEing
The Power to BE
Is living Heaven on Earth

Rise up!

Rise tall!

Come on,
Rise to your potential!

You are
Called to

Rise now!

In LOVE, we Trust

In LOVE, we hold Faith

In LOVE, we Believe

BEfore I Leave You

The State of BEcoming

At various points in time, people realize living an unsustainable life is not possible. It is a wake-up call, an internal flight for peace. Not understanding what this profound wave of undeniable need for change will bring, people are hoping for foundational happiness in their quest. Soon coming to light what this flight for peace brings, one is actioning their free will for Love. Finally. The goal before us is to BEcome, in the purest form, the Godly Essence that we are already. We resemble Christ in all that we humanly say, do and act. It isn't about being perfect. It is about being balanced. Understanding our path is about healing, expanding, elevating, and nurturing our infinite awareness of this process I am describing. So, when we stumble upon parts of us that don't resemble the light, we are required to pick ourselves up with LOVE. Applying the Law of Forgiveness is the ultimate act in SELF_LOVE. We don't judge ourselves when approaching a fork in the road before us. Everything is Divinely guided and prescribed by the Heavens as per our Soul's contact predetermined before arriving on Earth.

Sacred healing is a process of cleansing the soul. A purifying means capturing a deeper understanding of the authentic Self (YOU), un-layering the most profound Truth. It requires patience, persistence and, most of all, LOVE. Sometimes this process makes us uncomfortable to varying degrees as we embrace our suffering. Accepting the pain allows one to move past it onto a peaceful state. Developing trust within ourselves that we are capable of healing from this pain, the pain we have held onto for a very long time. Most of the time, our minds don't know where God is taking us as God leads us through sacred healing. It is a process of trusting God, and understanding the uncertainty is a prerequisite to achieving Peace. Through the uncertainty, we learn not to focus on the uncertainty but instead on the end peace that is coming; this is the state of BEcoming in action: learning to TRUST, have FAITH and BELIEVE in YOU_GOD producing SELF_LOVE.

Living through the sacred healing process breeds confidence as we learn to relinquish control. We do not control the healing process as the ego plays no part in healing; instead, the ego is what we are healing. We do not use the ego to heal itself. Instead, we actively engage the Divine Healing Energy to facilitate the sacred healing process - freeing our spirits from the grips of our egos and transmuting the ego into the Divine image. Each time we heal in this way, we elevate our souls. We become stronger as we ascend closer to God because as we heal our spirits, our spirits amalgamate within our Souls. Our Souls get bigger, brighter, and God-like, then eventually, our Souls unite with God, transmuting into our Holy Selves.

As I describe this Heavenly process from a bird's eye view, the journey starts in the present moment and all the individual moments that follow the first; paying attention to each moment as you live life starts the process. This sacred journey takes you through a self-discovery process of *Igniting, Embracing* and E*mbodying your truth*, one step at a time. This Holy Path is individual and interconnected to those around you, as prescribed by the Heavens. Any degree of peace experienced from reading this sacred poetry book is a compilation of little steps getting you to a deeper understanding of your authentic Self. This Sacred Poetry Book is a continuation of YOUr sacred evolution of Self moving you on your spiritual quest for the sustainable happiness you deserve.

Always with LOVE from ME to YOU, ME_YOU

Agatha

Know YOUr Worth and Stay Within IT

Layers of God's LIGHT working together for the greater good of YOU. BEcoming is an exercise expressed in union with GOD and not apart from IT. YOUr more significant part of you already knows this exercise and wants to be expressed in this way on Earth. GOD's LOVE for humanity transcends all hardships. When we learn to engage with LOVE, we begin to trust, have faith and believe in the sacred bond we already carry. This sacred bond allows us to apply the Law of Forgiveness. Forgiveness is the highway, a direct path to attaining YOU.

Taking Back YOUr Right to Live Heaven on Earth

Note to Reader

This image was given to me on December 19, 2021, as I was facing the sun shining bright before me. Feeling the warmth within me, God speaking directly through me, drawing onto paper, teaching me the concept of SELF Worth. God was inviting me forward with ITs depth of Love, security, calmness and peace as IT facilitated my forgiveness healing in this moment and all moments afterwards. I am guided to share this image as an invitation to you, as it was for me. God is present within you: activating your life through your thoughts, words, and actions. It is up to you to pay attention to this invitation and consciously decide whether to accept it or not. It is that simple.

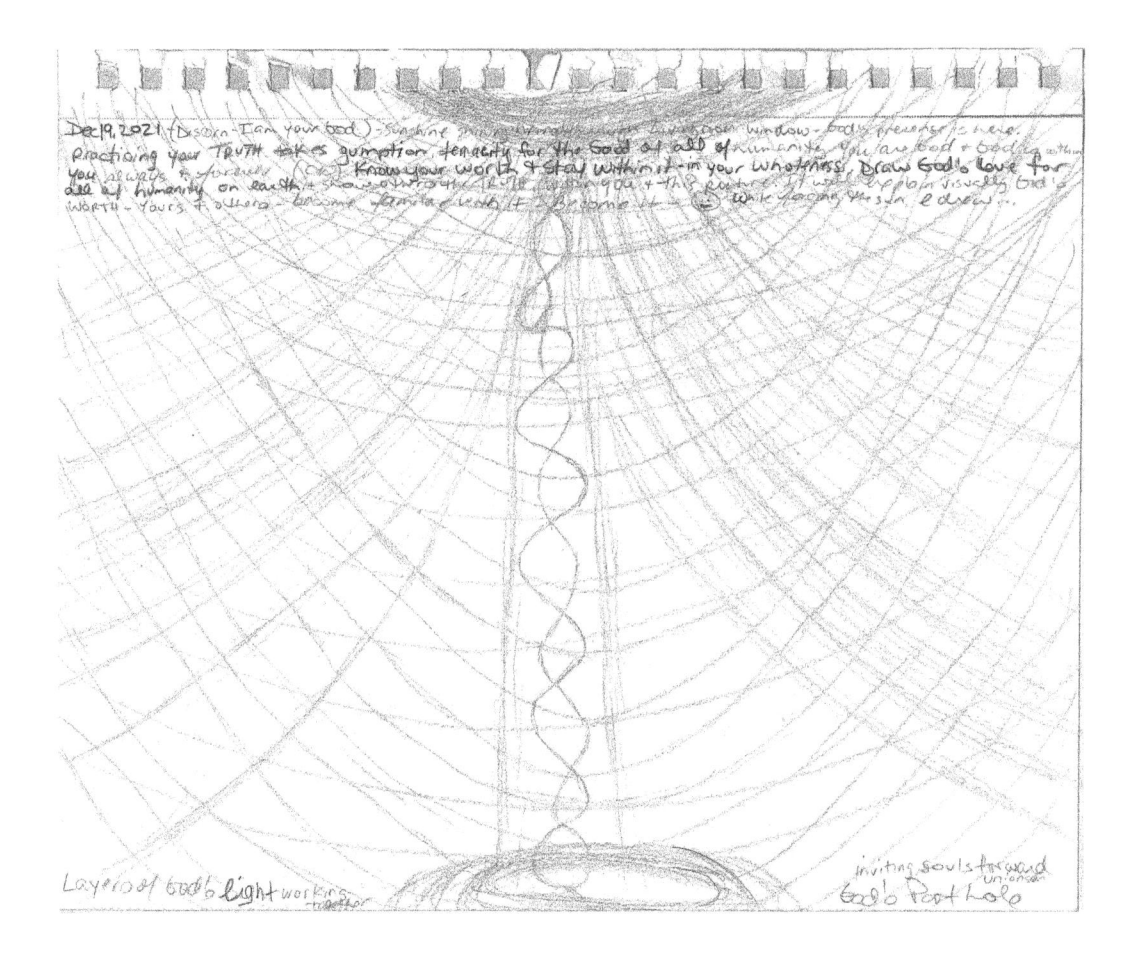

Dec 19, 2021 (Desoxn - I am your God) - sunshine through window - God's presence is here. Practicing your TRUTH takes gumption, tenacity for the God of all of humanity. You are God & God is within you always & forever ⟲ I know your world & stay within it - in your wholeness. Draw God's love for all of humanity on earth & know & trust God is with you & this picture it will explain visually God's WORTH - yours & others - become familiar with it & become it ☺ While doing this in I drew...

Layers of God's light working together

inviting souls forward in union
God's Port hole

Taking Back YOUr Right to Live Heaven on Earth

With Joy and Gratitude from my heart to yours,

Trusting and believing in yourself fosters faith of the unimaginable kind by the mind, but your Spirit already knows of the Sacred Bond you hold with GOD.

Thank you to all readers for sharing your sacred space with me as you read through this Book.

Expressing my SELF_LOVE in this way has been a healing journey I will not forget, for it has allowed me to travel deeper into myself. I know IT will touch YOUr heart in a way that is special just for YOU. I'm honoured to be part of your journey.

Peace BE with you.

Always and forever,

Agatha

BE. here. now.

The LOVE between you and me
Arches over our existence
Linking us to each other
A pathway of truth
Sharing Divine Light along it
Makes us grounded
As we strive to BE IT

BEcoming with ME
As you BE in every moment
Transcendence continues here

www.empoweringpractices.ca

@empowering_practices

@empoweringpractices

empowering practices